TRIBALISM

The Curse of 21st Century America

TRIBALISM

The Curse of 21st Century America

Michael C. Anderson

SBPC

SIMMS BOOKS PUBLISHING CORPORATION

SBPC

SIMMS BOOKS PUBLISHING CORP.

Publishers Since 2012

Published by Simms Books Publishing Corporation

Jonesboro, GA

Library of Congress Cataloging in Publication Data

2019915385

Michael C. Anderson

TRIBALISM: The Curse of 21st Century America

ISBN:978-0-9996882-2-9

Printed in the United States of America

Edited by Mary Hoekstra

Book Arrangement by Simms Books Publishing

Cover by Shelly M. Anderson/ Urias Brown

Dedication

To the American people who need to understand
what is happening.

Acknowledgement

I wish to thank:

Mary Hoekstra, my tireless and ruthless editor, who always challenges me to be the best.

James Simms, my publisher, for his interest and support.

My photographer Ellen Loeffler-Kalinowski.

Jordan Peterson for helping me understand the attack on freedom of speech.

Stephen Hicks for making sense out of Postmodernism and its weaknesses.

TABLE OF CONTENTS

Dedication i

Acknowledgements ii

Preface iii

1 Introduction 1

2 Converging Forces: Identity Politics,
Postmodernism, Tribalism 13

3 The Enlightenment 29

4 The Counter-Enlightenment 51

5 The Modern Age 69

6 History of Collectivism 93

7 The Fall of Socialism 119

8 The Death of Reason 147

9 Postmodernism 161

10 Postmodernism in America 179

11 The Damage 199

12 A Perspective on America Tribalism 229

13 Moral Capital 253

14 The Way forward 269

Glossary 289

Bibliography 297

Index 309

PREFACE

After publishing *The Progressive Gene* in November 2017, I started working on a companion book called, *The Conservative Gene*. My thinking behind the second book was to present the genetic foundations of the morality of the Right, which would build upon my previous work.

I had finished a substantial portion of *The Conservative Gene* when I stopped abruptly. The cause was a feeling of distraction after watching Jonathan Haidt being interviewed by Jordan Peterson. I knew Jonathan Haidt, of course, because he stimulated me to write *The Progressive Gene*, but I had no prior exposure to Peterson. I started watching more Peterson videos and got interested in his message of free speech rights and the corruption of free speech on college campuses. Peterson became universally known for his refusal to abide by an Ontario Provincial law requiring the public to use a new set of transgender pronouns rather than the traditional gender-based pronouns. Peterson refused to utilize words mandated by government.

I became interested in Peterson's views on Postmodernism. He blamed Postmodernism and Neo-Marxism for the corruption of Humanities and Social Science departments at elite universities. He believes that Postmodernism is a nihilistic ideology, intended to tear down Western intellectual traditions. Although I don't completely agree with Peterson's link between Postmodernism and Neo-Marxism, I was interested in his message and decided to research the role of Postmodernism in America today.

During my time in college, I spent two years in graduate school studying philosophy. I was a thesis short of a master's degree when I decided to make a career change into a more practical discipline. That was a time in the early 1970s, when Postmodernism was just getting started, but as I moved forward with my career, I retained an interest in philosophy and followed the evolution of Postmodernism into the 21st Century. I started putting my thoughts together and came to understand the importance of the link between

Postmodernism and the tribal society that exists in America today. This tribalist mentality is harmful because, when opposing parties are not talking, there is a low probability that the great problems America faces will be solved. So, I was driven to do the research required to understand the dynamics of Tribalism and write a book about it.

As I started working on the book, I searched for recent studies on Postmodernism and found Stephen Hicks' book *Explaining Postmodernism* quite interesting. Hicks did an excellent job of explaining Postmodernism, its place in the history of philosophy, and its impact on the 21st Century. Hicks does not discuss Tribalism, but there are three chapters in his book that provide context to the factors that have influenced it; the Climate of Collectivism, the Crisis of Socialism, and the Collapse of Reason.

I began to think about the changes in our society over the last two decades; secularization of Christmas, expanding identity politics, LGBTQ rights, and same-sex marriage. These and other changes in the American society have pushed our country into a tribal-like behavior, pitting the political parties against each other. The media enjoys the controversy and exploits it to increase their profits.

More recently, troubling trends on college campuses have reached the mainstream news. Conservative speakers are being denied the right to speak, and words like micro-aggressions, and safe spaces have made their way onto the front pages of newspapers. When I read that Brown University had constructed a safe-space environment where students could blow bubbles and use play-doh, I was flabbergasted. How could such nutty logic have taken over our college campuses? Why would anyone think that protecting young people from the real world was a good thing? What happens to those students after they graduate as wimps?

The United States is now a country of tribes, Left and Right, and it's scary to contemplate what this could turn into. The federal government is paralyzed. All political battles are special interest group against special interest group and no one is paying attention to the issues that really matter; the budget deficit, entitlements, health care, and education, to name a few. I determined to dig into this issue and write about it; to get the word out to all who are interested in learning more.

This subject of tribalism leads to questions that need to be answered. What are the forces that made us tribal? Assuming tribalism is bad, how do we get back to a time when we can communicate and debate ideas freely? What are the risks of America continuing in a tribal state?

The time for action is now. Clearly, we are not moving forward and continuing to ignore the danger we face would be a serious mistake.

CHAPTER ONE

INTRODUCTION

America faces many problems today, but there is one that rises above the rest, cuts across the entire society, and damages the psyche of the American people. That problem is Tribalism. Wittingly or unwittingly, Americans have become divided by ideology and political affiliation, gender, and race. This phenomenon emerged during the last decades of the 20th Century and accelerated after the year 2000. Its rise was propelled by several factors, including the eroding of American traditions, lifestyle changes due to increased communications, the global economy, the collapse of Socialism, and the Postmodernist attack on the concept of

"Modern".

Long accepted American traditions began to erode in the 1960s, following the falsely idealistic decade of the 1950s. Civil rights and anti-Viet Nam War protests highlighted the country's inequality and the government's foolish adventure in South East Asia. The second wave of Feminism took off, as women sought to get out of the house, pursue careers and become real stakeholders in society. The divorce rate skyrocketed, and families broke apart. Mass print and radio marketing, along with television, bombarded the nation with images of how Americans were supposed to live in order to get ahead. The 1990s brought us the internet and wireless phones, making communications ubiquitous. By the turn of the 21st Century, people became less involved with religion and secular themes appeared across the media.

The growth in Globalism and Internationalization followed the collapse of the Berlin Wall in 1989. Driven by Capitalist principles, it threatens to homogenize cultural uniqueness and destroy individuality, by creating the potential for large numbers of jobs to be lost, and the working class become disenfranchised.

Socialism collapsed for the final time as the Left's favorite ideology in 1989. Left thinkers were forced to accept the corrupt ideal that Socialist regimes represented. The collapse of Socialism robbed the Left of an ideology which could be used to counter Capitalist/Liberal tradition, so the Left shifted tactics and began to attack Capitalism directly.

In the 1970s, a group of French philosophers, emerging from the post-structural movement of the prior decade, introduced an *Avant garde* belief system that brought something completely new to a tired modern world. Postmodernists attacked the Enlightenment, claiming that late 20th Century America had transitioned from a modern to a postmodern society. This dogma gained enormous popularity because it appeared to describe all that was happening and all that was wrong with an American society nearing the end of the 20th Century.

Postmodernism is a belief system structured to criticize and tear down, without offering a replacement. It is anti-Enlightenment to the core, staking out the position that all humans have accomplished in the last two hundred years was based on power relationships and is now obsolete.

Tribalism

The fall of the Berlin Wall in 1989 ended the Left-Right battle over world domination and left a void in its place. What ideology would replace it to become the focus of global political opposition? In America, there was a radical split about how our country should operate and be governed. Progressives on the left created a new understanding of society built around Postmodernism. That view was resisted by the Conservative Right. Both sides were reacting against a new world that seemed uncomfortable and alien.

The turn of the 21st Century saw Tribalism in America accelerate. The Clinton impeachment, the first election of George Bush with its controversy, the terrorist attacks of 9/11, and the Iraq and Afghan wars divided the country. The Federal government became more polarized as those in the ideological middle, from both parties, were replaced with those who were more extreme. Mass media continued to produce an explosion of information of dubious quality, and the burgeoning social media phenomenon allowed people to have a voice, no matter how radical or truthful their words might be. Somewhere along the way, Americans became more sensitive to "trigger words," even if uttered in private. Political correctness, which began demanding strict

4

adherence and sensitivity to the disadvantaged, rose to a visceral level. Confusion about what it means to be an American drove our people to the safety of the tribe where they felt comfortable among those that shared their point of view.

As we near the end of the second decade of the 21st Century, no position or idea is out of bounds if it meets the objective of furthering an ideology. According to extremists at both ends of the political spectrum, truth doesn't matter. It's all about winning the ideological battle and the power that flows from it. This is particularly true of those on the Left, who hate Trump and his disruption of their agenda. His personality and success are open sores, and his enemies have been irrationally engaged in engineering his downfall since he announced his intention to run for president. The Right is not blameless because its reactionary behavior to the Postmodern world has spawned a new tendency toward xenophobia, racism, and violence.

The Tribalism gripping our nation is a sign of decay due to the loss of "moral capital"; the principles and beliefs that have held Americans together for two hundred years. These beliefs include family, local community, moral community, and country. Moral capital unites Americans and makes them feel good about their lives. When moral capital erodes away, the people become tribal.

The family unit has changed significantly from the days of the working husband and stay at home wife. Even the definition of marriage itself has changed. The necessity for two-parent incomes makes life more stressful. Kids go to daycare and spend less time with their parents. Technology has had an impact on neighborhoods and communities by giving people reasons to stay home. They can use their computer, TV, or phone to communicate, instead of talking to the neighbor next door or attending a community event. Staying home means less socializing with others, less communication and less sharing of ideas. At home, family members have a variety of ways to interact with others online, instead of spending time communicating within the family.

Participation in organized religion has decreased in importance in recent years. More people claim they are not religious and church attendance has declined. Churches, like communities and neighborhoods, have always been a source of connectivity between people.

Last and perhaps most important, the national connection that has always flowed from sharing pride in our country has been damaged. The lack of effectiveness of government and the influence of lobbyists have stifled America's progress. Congress is more polarized than ever, and corruption has tarnished the image of elected officials. Questionable wars have caused great division in the country and destroyed thousands of lives.

Historically, events that have threatened the whole country have brought us together. The larger the threat, the closer we get. These events have been absent recently, the last being the 9/11 attacks. The unity that flowed from that event was dissipated by controversy over the Iraq and Afghan wars. The second Bush term and both Obama terms marked a continuing movement toward disunity.

Postmodernism feeds into and contributes to the fragmentation that exists in America today. It opposes any universalizing principles, like religion or nation, it questions truth, and exercises its ability to divide our nation.

Format of this book
The book begins with a summary of our tribal state and then

proceed to a detailed discussion of the forces that came together in the late 20th Century to produce tribalism.

Chapter Two, Converging Forces, explains how American Tribalism has resulted from changes in the modern world, identity politics, and the emergence of Postmodernism. Postmodernism was able to inject itself into the mindset of the Left when Socialism failed, and the Left lost its favorite ideology.

Chapter Three, The Enlightenment, traces Enlightenment history and how it set the stage for the development of the modern world. One of the factors behind the emergence of Tribalism is the attack on the founding principles of the Enlightenment.

Chapter Four, The Counter-Enlightenment, provides a description of the historical opposition to the Enlightenment. The Counter-Enlightenment stood in strong opposition during the time when the Enlightenment was emerging, but its criticism had its greatest impact in the late 20th Century.

Chapter Five, The Modern Age, describes the changes in Western society resulting from the Enlightenment. It is the modern age that gave us capitalism, democracy, and science.

Chapter Six, The History of Collectivism, describes a counter-movement, that emerged alongside the Enlightenment. It asserted that political systems designed around group interests bring more value to human society than the Enlightenment focus on individual interests. The Collectivist model led to the development of the Socialist ideologies, which had a significant impact on the 20th Century.

Chapter Seven, The Failure of Socialism, describes the failure of Collectivist thinking as it relates to building a political system superior to the Capitalist model. The 20th Century showed that the Socialist model was unworkable and impractical as a real political solution. The failure of Socialism produced a split in the ideology of the Left, moving some to embrace Postmodernism, and others identity politics.

Chapter Eight, Describes The Collapse of Reason; the failure of arguments about truth and knowledge which marked the end of a two-hundred-year debate among philosophers who favored and opposed the Enlightenment. After the mid-20th Century, philosophers began to believe it impossible to prove what is real outside of the sense data we use to perceive the world.

Chapter Nine, Postmodernism, introduces the Postmodernist philosophy, including its origins and basic principles, and features the profiles of three of its founders.

Chapter Ten, The Road to Postmodernism in America, describes the establishment of Postmodernism into American Academia, where it has had a significant impact on Humanities and Social Science departments. By the turn of the 21st Century, Postmodernism had become well-established as the principle philosophical system in Humanities departments at elite universities.

Chapter Eleven, The Damage, discusses the impact of Tribalism on the American society. This damage is measured by its impact on American politics, higher education, where Postmodernism supports the rejection of Enlightenment principles, and in society as a whole, which is exposed to the polarization of political ideology.

Chapter Twelve, A Perspective on American Tribalism, provides historical examples of Tribalism in Europe and in the United States.

Chapter Thirteen, Moral Capital, is a measure of how well morality holds a society together. These factors include family, local community, moral community, and patriotism. Although patriotism is a relatively recent addition, the other three have existed as long as man has lived in groups. When moral capital becomes degraded due to the disruption of society's norms or changes in human behavior, it creates anxiety among groups and fosters tribalism.

Chapter Fourteen, The Way Forward, suggests how America can move away from Tribalism and back to a more cooperative society. Tribalism is ultimately destructive to any political system infected by it, so the damage it causes can reach a point of no return. The tribes must find a way to settle their differences for the benefit of all, because the stability of the American political system and the welfare of its people are more important than petty disagreements about ideology.

This book seeks to explain the forces causing Tribalism, which are mostly hidden from the American people. We hear words like "male privilege" and are not sure where they came from and why they rose to headline status. It's important for every American to understand the uncontrolled efforts of the political extremists, who are damaging our way of life. Those extremists are driven by a desire to capture and maintain power. We must return to a time when the power goals of the politicians match the needs of the American people, so we all can benefit.

CHAPTER TWO

CONVERGING FORCES: The Late Modern World, Identity Politics, And Postmodernism.

I know that if we allow ourselves into the gridlock of Tribalism, we're in trouble.

Elizabeth Lesser

To understand the causes of Tribalism in the United States, one must start by reviewing European and American history from 1650 to the present day. The year 1650 marked the beginning of the Enlightenment Project, which led to permanent changes in Western society; its institutions, governments, and the power of its people. In the mid - 20th

Century, changes in Western society set the stage for an attack on Enlightenment principles and created the environment for Tribalism to proliferate.

This chapter provides that history in summary, including a discussion of the social forces that led to the Tribalism we see today. In the following eight chapters, we provide the details needed to complete that story. Then, starting with Chapter Eleven, we assess the damage Tribalism has done to the American society and how we might expect this curse to resolve itself.

Man's formation of tribes

To better understand Tribalism, take a moment and think about the word "tribe" in human history. Mankind's first grouping was the band, which was his most common social organization up to the time of the Neolithic Period (10,000-3,000 BC). Bands were a loose connection of 30-100 people with some marriage relationships, no hierarchy, and living in a flat egalitarian society. The band was held together by primary kinship associations in the group. Its structure was defined by the male line, required marriage outside the group (probably to minimize genetic defects), and located a married couple near the husband's parents.

At some point, the need arose for a more complex human society and mankind formed tribes. The early tribes were groups of bands, who came together out of mutual interest. Then, as the tribal concept matured, they began to consolidate. Consolidation meant organizational efficiency and leadership; both valuable when coming into conflict with other tribes. The leader was the chief, who served as an advisor, rather than supreme leader, so important decisions were made by a consensus vote of the members. Internal elements within the tribe created commonality; external elements centered around the means of protection from other tribes. These elements were the "glue" that held the tribe together. In America today, groups have retreated to a tribal level because the higher levels of commonality have broken down.

A Tribal Example in History

The Roman civilization was founded when three Latin tribes came together to form an association. Once the association became strong enough and the population grew to a size that required a more complex organization, Rome became a monarchy. As Rome expanded, new tribes formed or were brought into the existing society. Members of those new tribes were designated as second class (Plebeians) citizens and were not given the same status as the original tribes (Patricians). The Roman monarchy ended when the last king was deposed and Rome became a Republic. As it grew, the Republic matured as a political system, and the concept of tribe decreased in importance.

In the early period of the Republic, the Patricians used their hereditary position, wealth, positions in government, and control over the legal system to keep power over the lower class. Over time, however, wealthy class decided to share power with the Plebeians and this gradual effort helped maintain stability in the Republic. Near the end of the Republican Period, Rome became tribal again as political factions formed tribes and fought against each other for the loyalty of the people. Eventually, this new tribal state made the Republic unstable enough to create an opening for a military leader to use the loyalty of the army to take power.

The emergence of Tribalism in America is the result of attacks on Enlightenment in the second half of the 20th Century. The concept of Modern, which had been the sociological basis of Western Civilization since the Enlightenment, was criticized for being out of touch with late 20th Century American society. The Tribalism in

America today is political and social. The tribes are defined by their political affiliation; each party representing a faction in the war for and against Capitalism.

Historical forces influencing American Tribalism

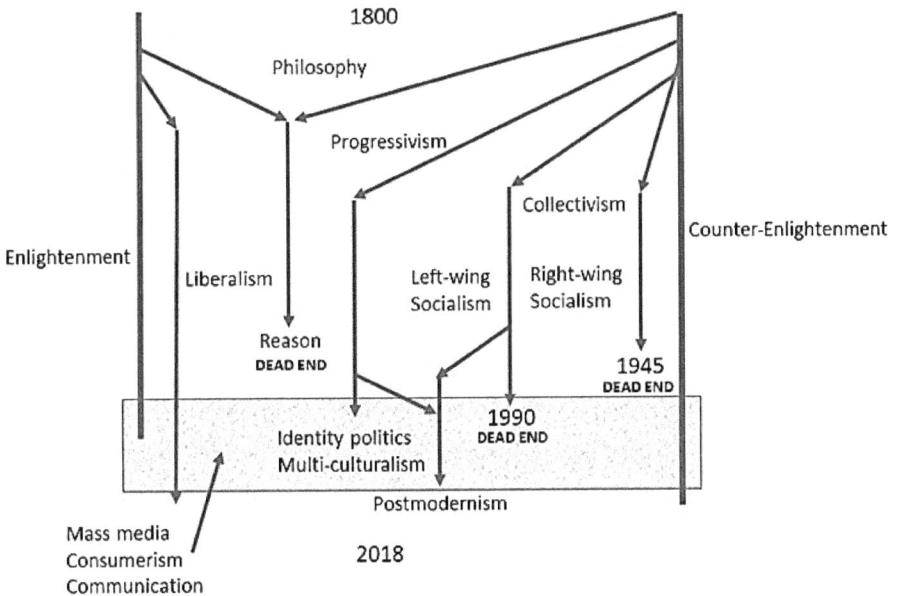

The chart above lays out in graphical form the historical forces that, when combined with the changes in American society in the second half of the 20th Century, led to Tribalism in the United States.

The Enlightenment

The Enlightenment has been the major intellectual and cultural focus in the West since 1800 and is responsible for the principle ideas that define the Modern World. The Counter-Enlightenment was an attack on and criticism of the Enlightenment by conservative elements who saw it as breaking too strongly with religious and secular traditions. Criticism of the Enlightenment began to accelerate after 1970.

The Enlightenment created the Modern World in which; science, religious freedom, and Capitalism flourished. Its focus on individualism tore down old political models and made government the servant of man. Science created technology, which spawned the Industrial Revolution, and brought affordable goods to Western society. Capitalism defined the form of business which would deliver technology efficiently.

Collectivism

Collectivist thinking was a key competitor to the Enlightenment from the beginning. Jean Jacques Rousseau, and others after him, asserted that human society functioned best when it was organized around groups rather than individuals. In Rousseau's view, the Enlightenment was dangerous because it allowed the corrupted man to control his own destiny. What was needed was a middle ground between primitive man and Modern society. This middle ground would employ religion as the tool to keep man under control. The Collectivist model would later form the basis of both Left-wing and Right-wing Socialism.

Right and Left Socialism

Socialism had been the principle competitor to Liberalism since the end of the Enlightenment period, but by the end of the 20th Century, its supporters had to accept the reality that it failed as a political system. The fall of Nazi Germany and the Soviet Union ended a long series of attempts to make Socialism work, but its economic and social ideals could never be achieved. Socialism's failure created a void for the political Left who had now lost their socio-political ideology. In response, some on the Left moved to embrace identity politics. Others cast about for an alternative.

Collapse of Reason

The Collapse of Reason occurred, in the middle of the 20th Century, when philosophical debate about the way to attain knowledge reached a dead end. To some this meant that truth was unattainable. Postmodernists agreed that truth was dead based on their view that all ideas were a social construction.

Progressivism in the United States

The Progressive Movement began in the late 19th Century as a reaction against worker exploitation and corrupt politics. Once a strong program of Theodore Roosevelt, it was adopted by Democrats during the time Wilson was president. Dormant in the 1920s, its popularity reemerged in the 1930s as part of Franklin Roosevelt's New Deal program. Later, Roosevelt changed his allegiance from Progressives and unions to big business in order to fund his vision of the welfare state. By 1950, Progressivism was dead and American Liberalism had replaced it.

America in Transition

Post-World War II America experienced an entirely new reality, based on a changing economy, lifestyle, and modes of communication. There was an unprecedented period of growth following the end of the war, based on the transition of a significant share of industrial production toward consumer goods. In the Fifties, the spectacle of excess conspicuous consumption, once regarded by the older morality as a sign of sin, had become a sign of status.

Television, advertising, and consumerism became a way of life for the growing American middle class. Apart from concerns over the Cold War, the 1950s were a period of optimism and consumption.

By the 1960s, everything had changed. The American culture became fragmented over the Viet Nam War and society seemed to be breaking down. The sexual revolution overturned traditional moral views, women sought recognition and equal rights with men, and African-Americans fought for equality with white America. The broadcast of the events surrounding the assassination of President Kennedy, the murder of Lee Harvey Oswald, and Kennedy's funeral shocked Americans into a new reality of immediate exposure to violence.

With the sense of alienation, confusion, and disagreement that existed in America, the door was open for new ideas to emerge.

Identity Politics and Multiculturalism

New Left programs begun during the Viet Nam Era were a Progressive "false start." The Progressives would not appear in the open again until the Liberal welfare state ideology was discarded. That is not to say Progressives weren't operating after 1960; they had always embraced Socialism and freely adopted its attack model against Capitalism. Criticism of wealth, protection of the environment, and promotion of multiculturalism were key areas on which Progressives focused.

Sparked by the Civil Rights Movement, identity politics, and the influx of immigrants from Latin America and Asia, multiculturalism emerged to challenge Modern Liberalism as an ideological solution for creating diversity in America. Liberalism had never tried to address the merging of identities and looked at America as a melting pot that would blend immigrants into our social fabric. Consequently, when Liberalism became tarnished by the failed welfare state experience, multiculturalism was able to move forward.

Multiculturalism repudiated Nativism (protecting the interests of native born) and put itself at odds with the harmonizing nature of a variegated yet united national identity. Scholars have argued that extreme cultural fragmentation disorients people, preventing them from locating themselves in history, grasping the shape of a nation's history, and understanding the right way to live within it. This disconnect has been an additional catalyst in the formation of Tribalism.

Postmodernism

In the late 1970s, Postmodernism emerged as a new philosophical approach addressing the changing society at the end of the 20th Century. It asserted that the Modern Era was dead, and the Postmodern period had replaced it. The ideas and narratives of the Enlightenment were now obsolete. The Postmodern world was critical of the validity of truth since truth was generated traditionally by those in power.

Postmodernism became attractive because it seemed to accurately describe the realities of the late 20th Century. A large portion of the Left adopted it as a replacement for Socialism. It was readily absorbed into American academia and reformed many of the disciplines within the Social Sciences and the Humanities. Some new Postmodernism-driven disciplines emerged that made no contribution to the expansion of human knowledge, like Gender Studies, but their creation was justified based on advancing social justice ideologies.

Postmodernism was comfortable in the middle of chaos. It helped drive Tribalism by way of an emphasis on fragmentation, anti-universalism, and power relationships. It also brought into question the ability of democracy to tolerate cultural differences. Currently, identity groups are critical of today's political climate when it does not recognize their characteristics and discounts their unique contribution. Tribalism is also deeply embedded in New Social movements, which support a multicultural society.

Tribalism today

The Tribalism we see today is unhealthy for America. We observe election cycles of alternating administrations that, predictably, dedicate themselves to reversing the accomplishments of the last administration. Any efforts to move the country forward take a back seat to the reversals, which must come first. The end goal of each party is to destroy its opponent, so it may pursue a permanent majority; so, gone are the days of working together within the system. Tribalism is attractive because it requires little thought. If you know what side you're on, you just listen for updates from within your tribe and move along through life. Your view is never threatened because you never venture outside the bubble. You see the other tribe as evil and swear you'll never risk being disloyal by communicating with them or giving credence to any of their positions. When a member of the rival tribe criticizes you, you deflect by bringing up one of their shortcomings. This is the technique the Soviets used during the Cold War. When confronted with the inhuman killing that was part of their system, they replied by drawing attention to racial strife in the United States as the great American flaw. That tactic is now employed in our homeland. [1]

Operating in the tribal echo chamber generates more extreme positions over time. The word "hate," for example, has now become a one-stop replacement for a whole spectrum of milder emotions that once described disagreements between people. Now you might be engaging in "hate speech" if you defend your religious beliefs against homosexuality. Fifty years ago, the term "white supremacist", described advocates and practitioners of bigotry. Now the term is routinely used on the Left to simply mean inequality in a multicultural America. This broadening of a definition implies there is no difference between America today and

---

[1] Andrew Sullivan, *America Wasn't Built for Humans*. (New York Magazine: September 18, 2017).

America in the 1830s and negates all the progress that has been made since then.

The greatest threat to a politician today is not the candidate from the opposing party but a more ideologically extreme election primary opponent. The removal of incentives for cross-tribal compromise strengthens those for tribal extremism. We saw this in the elections of 2016 and 2018 when experienced Liberals had trouble defeating some far-Left Progressives.

Hypocrisy is rampant and obvious in the political parties. The Left won't say "Islamic terrorist" or "illegal immigrant." The Right won't admit that trickle-down economics doesn't work, or our defense expenditures are too large. To the Left, inappropriate sex is tolerated if it's done by their candidate, but not the other side's candidate. Those on the Left often fight among themselves over their own issues. One faction wants wind power, but another will not allow birds to be killed by the propellers. Those on the Right want to cut welfare programs first, before all else, and let the market decide who is driven into poverty.

In 2011, a poll reported that only 30 percent of white

Evangelicals believed that private immorality was irrelevant for public life. In 2018, that same poll reported that the number had skyrocketed to 72 percent, since their candidate had moved into the White House.[2]

When a party leader in a Liberal democracy proposes a shift in direction, there is usually an internal debate which can go on for years. For decades, a defining foreign-policy concern for Republicans was their suspicion of the Soviet Union. When a tribal leader demands a shift in direction, the tribe immediately jumps to the leader's command. The Republicans went from free trade to protectionism, and from internationalism to nationalism, almost overnight.

Tribalism is well entrenched and will be with us for a while. One imagines that when it reaches some extreme point, there will be a rebound toward normalcy. It remains to be seen if and when that will happen.

POINTS TO REMEMBER

---

[2] Public Religion Research Institute. *White Evangelical Support for Trump at an All-time High.* (PRRI, April 18, 2018).

- Tribalism in America traces its creation to a variety of factors, including rapid changes to American, society, the collapse of Socialism as a political force, the Left's embrace of identity politics, and the influence of Postmodernism on American academia.

- The defeat of the American Left in the mid-Seventies was not only the context for the shift from social analysis to cultural studies, but also for a new affiliation between the political Left and Postmodernism.

- Postmodernists vigorously attacked the Left, dwelling on the repressive side of the welfare state and labor-centered Left, seeing their Enlightenment baggage as the source of a variety of problems such as socio-cultural exclusion, soulless regimentation, and homogenization of society.

- The major political parties in America have moved farther apart over recent decades because the middle ground of moderate ideology has disappeared. The parties have become as tribal as the constituents they represent.

CHAPTER THREE

THE ENLIGHTENMENT

The Enlightenment put the individual on a pedestal and gave him Science, Capitalism, and Democracy to play with.
Unknown

In the history of Western mankind, the Enlightenment was perhaps its most profound and far-reaching intellectual advance. Centered in Europe, the Enlightenment fostered the ideas that defined the Modern world, became the foundation of the American political system and played a role in the development of Tribalism in 21st Century America.

After 150 years as the standard for the way man should live in society, the Enlightenment became a target for those who saw a disconnect between it and the Postmodern world of the 1970s. Critics asserted the disconnect was real because the world was operating at a faster pace than at any time in its history. The new modern age felt different, somehow, than previous times. That difference helped launch the Postmodernist philosophy as a critic of Liberal/Capitalist America. Today, we remain locked in a battle to determine whether the Enlightenment was obsolete or merely evolving.

The Enlightenment was a social and intellectual movement in Europe and North America between 1650-1800. It was the period in Western history that brought a new focus on the individual as the primary agent for controlling human destiny. Previously, people had been told what to think by their church and their king, who claimed exclusive access to the will of God and an exclusive grasp of the way to live a moral life. Knowledge was hoarded by the elites, leaving the common man with no way to determine the truth for himself. The Enlightenment swept aside the right of the powerful to control the individual, and this new found freedom set the stage for the emergence of science, Capitalism, and

Democracy as foundations for the advancement of the human species.

From the standpoint of science, the Enlightenment is divided into two parts: the early (1650-1750), and late (1750-1800). The early Enlightenment was characterized by the advent of science and the belief that truth could be determined by intuition. The Late Enlightenment decarded the value of intuition after the philosopher David Hume attacked the notion of the reliability of the senses and their ability to accurately describe the real world. Hume destroyed the rationalist ideology and forced science to redefine itself. That redefinition, the modern scientific method, based on a consensus about science's theoretical foundation, survives to the present day.

The Enlightenment was not a homogeneous movement with a single goal. It was a set of overlapping intellectual movements, which influenced the entire range of human experience. It permeated every aspect of human life: religion, politics, economics, science, and most important, man's view of himself. A universally optimistic endeavor, based on the idea of progress, the Enlightenment was also a time and context for intellectual contemplation. For example, the seductive nature of free thought forced individuals to decide whether or not to live with the danger or consequence free thought could engender. That same freedom of thought is under attack today by those who claim it contains biases that unfairly favor certain groups over others. In their view, the bias can only be remediated by limiting the freedom of the offending groups.

New ideas lead us to technologies that produce great benefit, as long as man continues to remind himself of his moral responsibility. Science that cures, can also harm. Technology that enhances human thought and behavior can be addictive. During the Enlightenment, Western man decided his innate curiosity must be harnessed and put to work on the acquisition of all knowledge that was previously unknown. The benefits that would be gained from such an endeavor outweighed the risks of trying to tame the Universe. That question of science as a "good-harmful" agent is more significant today, than it was 200 years ago, because the risks are much greater now. One does not have to look much further than weapons of mass destruction and genetic engineering to see how mankind could destroy life on our planet.

Prelude to the Enlightenment

Monarchies were the preeminent political model from antiquity to the beginning of the Enlightenment period. They were successful in the pre-modern society because wealth created power and power was concentrated at the top of society. Monarchies were able to maintain their power through hereditary legitimacy.

The discovery of the Justinian code, in 1077 AD, legitimized the authoritarian monarchical state through sanctions provided to it by the Catholic Church. In the period that followed, monarchs were able to strengthen their alliances with the Papacy in ways that were mutually beneficial. The church received the political and military support it needed to protect its authority, and in return, the monarchs were designated as the official representatives of God on earth. The real world, consisted of everything and every person beneath the wealthy classes. That world was brutally unfair, populated as it was by a suffering poverty class, and a subsistence existence, at best, for almost everyone else. The majority had little opportunity to rise above their station.

In the 14th Century, Humanism ignited a new spark which began a focus on the inherent value of human life. This scholarly approach was centered on the analysis of ancient Latin and Greek texts as a way to revive scholarship. Humanists eventually produced two essential inputs to the Enlightenment which would follow: criticism of the intellectual wasteland of the times; and the calling out of abuses by and within the Catholic Church.

Petrarch (1304-74), considered the first Humanist, reacted against what he saw as human ignorance in the centuries preceding his birth, labeling that time "the Dark Ages." He sought to revive the ancient works of Cicero and return Europe to the intellectual rigor of antiquity.

Erasmus (1466-1536), who followed Petrarch a century later, was a Catholic priest, theologian and scholar who traveled widely across Europe. He studied the Bible and, based on his knowledge of Greek and Latin, was able to offer new interpretations of the sacred text, as well as translations into modern Latin and Greek. These translations gave the public direct access to the Bible, removing their dependency on the official church interpretation.[3] Although he retained

---

[3] Latin was still in use in Europe in the 16th century as the official language of the law. Government officials and scholars were able to read the Bible and interpret it for themselves.

his loyalty as a Catholic, Erasmus was highly critical of the Catholic super-structure and he suggested that it carve out a middle way in order to reform itself.

Despite being pushed to reform, the Church was unwilling to change and continued to violate principles that were part of its foundational belief system. Among its faults, the most egregious was the selling of indulgences. This practice allowed individuals to make monetary donations to the church to ensure God's forgiveness and guarantee their place in heaven. Public frustration with this policy led to the schism within the church that burgeoned into the Protestant Reformation.

During the period from 1517, when Martin Luther nailed his 95 theses to the cathedral door in Wittenberg, to 1648, when the Treaty of Westphalia ended the Thirty Years War, there was endless warring in Europe over religion. In those bloody decades, some eight million people lost their lives. The peace that followed, established Lutheranism and Calvinism as legitimate Protestant competitors to the Catholic Church and led to a spiritual retrenchment that helped break up the Holy Roman Empire.

As the Enlightenment took hold after 1700, the historical ties between the Catholic Church and the great monarchies of the West were broken forever. Monarchs were pressured to accept religious tolerance and separate their temporal authority from the spiritual and moral authority of the church. The Enlightenment defined new roles for monarchs who sought education for themselves and to demonstrate that their kingdoms were "enlightened."

Rational Thinking

In the early period of the Enlightenment, rationalist thinkers began to dominate philosophy and other academic disciplines including art, history, and science. Descartes (1596-1650), Spinoza (1632-1677), and Leibniz (1646-1716) were the main proponents of Rationalism, the philosophical view that human reasoning was the chief source and test of knowledge. More formally, Rationalism was a theoretical foundation upon which the criteria of truth were not sensory but were obtained by an internal thought process.

The Rationalists argued that certain truths existed without question, and human intellect could directly understand them. They asserted that certain rational principles existed in logic, mathematics, ethics, and metaphysics; those principles were so fundamentally true that denying them would be nonsensical. The Rationalists confidence in reason was so high they regarded empirical proofs and physical evidence as unnecessary in some cases. In other words, one could gain knowledge independently from sensory experience.

In the late 18th Century, a controversy arose over the conflict between Rationalism and a new philosophical discipline called Empiricism. David Hume (1711-1776), principal among Empiricists, asserted that knowledge comes from our perception of the world. Because that perception can be unreliable, absolute truth is indeterminate. There is no permanence to objects outside of our sense of them.

Immanuel Kant (1724-1804), considering Hume's theories, worked on solving the dispute during the 1780s. He put aside Rationalism and its proof of reality to analyze how human beings acquire knowledge. In the end, Kant decided humans could not know the real world because senses separated us from what is outside us. Moreover, Kant separated knowledge humans gained from their senses from knowledge they derived from things that are "in themselves." The concept of God is an example of a "thing in itself," not tied to sensory data, so it cannot be disproved.

The Rationalists were a tribe of traditionalists carrying forward ancient theories of knowledge. These theories did not work well in a world where science was able to demonstrate their flaws. The tribe of scientists who abandoned Rationalism in favor of the scientific method ended up winning the battle, but there were still debates about knowledge and perception that were left to the philosophers to think about.

Individualism

Enlightenment philosophers and scientists believed that Individualism was not only the awakening of the human spirit, but a belief in self-reliance. They also believed that the interests of a person should take precedence over the interests of the state and any group within it. Individualism started with the fundamental premise that the person was the vehicle to lead the human struggle for liberation; therefore, society had to be structured in a way that supported that goal. Classical Liberalism, Existentialism, and Anarchism are examples of historical movements that placed the individual at the center of society.

Science

Science, prior to the Enlightenment, was called Natural Philosophy and included the theoretical study of nature and the physical universe. Its companion discipline was Natural History, which involved qualitative and descriptive studies of objects in the world. During the Enlightenment, science emerged as a practical discipline in its own right, separate from philosophy. Its role was for individuals to gain knowledge from the real world, rather than just think about what it must be like.

Science was a foundational component of the Enlightenment, starting with Francis Bacon (1561-1626), who introduced the scientific method to the world. He argued that scientific knowledge should be based on inductive reasoning and careful observation of events in nature. Most important, he argued that knowledge could be achieved through use of a skeptical and methodical approach which would prevent scientists from misleading themselves. Even though his Baconian method and its practical ideas did not have a long-lasting influence, the idea of using a skeptical methodology made Bacon the father of the Scientific Method.

After Bacon came Descartes, Galileo (1564-1642), Isaac Newton (1643-1727), and others who made additional contributions to the development of science. These heroes of the Enlightenment created practical science as a replacement for philosophical inquiry; so, it became possible, for the first time, to design and manufacture products for the benefit of mankind.

- Galileo (1564-1642), invented the telescope in 1608 and made significant contributions to physics and astronomy.
- William Harvey (1578-1657), described the circulation of blood in 1628.
- Robert Hook (1635-1703), identified the cell as a unit of life in 1665.
- Robert Boyle (1627-1691), introduced his laws of chemical reactions also in 1665.
- Leeuwenhoek (1632-1723), discovered and described microorganisms for the first time in 1675.
- Newton published his *Principia Mathematica* which became the basis for modern physics in 1687.
- Zacharias Janssen (1585-1638), invented the microscope in 1590.

- Carl Linnaeus (1707-1778), published his work on the classification of plants and animals in 1735.

As science developed, it came under criticism. Traditionalists declared it had no value. The church and conservative forces attacked it as an attempt to replace God. Those attacks were ineffective and science was able to prove its value when technology (applied science) started changing human society.

Textile manufacturing became more efficient with the invention of weaving machines, which appeared in the first half of the 18th Century. Manufacturing of iron products was enhanced when producers switched from charcoal to coke and could produce higher furnace temperatures. The steam engine helped launch the Industrial Revolution. In the mid-18th Century, large scale production of chemicals was initiated and improved the efficiency of the production of glass, textiles, soap, and paper. Transportation was enhanced through the development of better canals and more efficient sails for ships, making them faster.

Political Theory and Liberalism
With the Enlightenment's emphasis on the individual, and

the move away from authoritarian governments and the traditional church, new ideas about political systems began to emerge. How would man govern himself, absent the old foundations? The Greeks had their democracy and the Romans had their republic, but these were considered historical anomalies during the time of the Enlightenment.

A new ideology we now label Classic Liberalism, emerged as a political form. Core beliefs of this new system established the idea of society as individuals, departing from the older views of society as a family. Classic Liberals believed that individuals should take the lead in determining how they could achieve success in life, and should also have a say in how their government is run. The Liberals were the new tribe, in opposition to the traditionalists who looked at society as a family. It would be another 100 years before Collectivism would rise from the writings of Rousseau to challenge the Liberals.

The philosopher Thomas Hobbes (1588-1679), stated the purpose of government should be to minimize conflicts between individuals that could not be resolved in a state of nature. An example of this would be a disagreement over property ownership. In a state of nature, two men might kill each other over control of a disputed piece of land. In a society, courts would settle that issue without violence. Hobbs also believed the best way to motivate humans was to create a financial incentive. Good pay for work performed would allow people to rise out of poverty and lessen the financial burden of government.

Classical Liberals also argued for what they called a "minimal state," limiting government to protecting individual rights, maintaining a common defense, and creating laws that would protect citizens from each other. They insisted that the rights of citizens should be negative in nature, meaning that constitutions should list rights that protected individuals and free markets from government interference.[4]

In the 17th Century, Liberal ideas began to influence governments in The Netherlands, Switzerland, England and Poland, but continued to be strongly opposed by those who favored absolute monarchy and established religion. Then, in the 18th Century, America became the first government

---

[4] Classical Liberals did not like democracy because citizen voting could harm property rights and the rule of law.

43

founded without a monarch or a hereditary aristocracy. The *American Declaration of Independence* included the well-known words, "all men are created equal; that they are endowed by their Creator with certain unalienable rights; that among these are life, liberty, and the pursuit of happiness; that to insure these rights, governments are instituted among men, deriving their just powers from the consent of the governed."[5] The American model of Liberalism eventually spread around the globe as a replacement for aristocratic power governments.

Capitalism

Drawing on ideas of Adam Smith (1723-1790), Classic Liberals believed that all individuals should be free to manage their own economic self-interests, and use that freedom for the creation of new businesses. An entrepreneur should be free to pursue any opportunity to create a business he felt he could bring to a level of profitability. Business owners should reap the benefits of their success or suffer a penalty if their business failed. Capital was the key to business operations. It took capital to start the business and, if it operated efficiently, the business would generate additional capital as profit for the owners.

---

[5] United States Declaration of Independence, (July 4, 1776).

Classic Liberals argued that individuals should be free to obtain work from the highest-paying employers. Consequently, the profit motive would ensure that the products people desired were produced at prices they could afford. In a free market, both labor and capital would receive the greatest possible reward, while consumer demand would be an impetus for organized efficient production.

Capitalism in its modern form can be traced to the emergence of Agrarian Capitalism and Mercantilism in the Renaissance during the mid-16th Century. Capital and commercial trade had existed since ancient times, but they did not lead to industrialization or dominate the production process of society. Modern Capitalism required a set of conditions, including specific technologies of mass production, the ability to independently and privately own and trade in means of production, a class of workers willing to sell their labor power for a living, a legal framework promoting commerce, a physical infrastructure allowing the circulation of goods on a large scale, and security for private accumulation. A considerable number of these conditions do not exist in some Third World countries even today, despite plenty of available capital and labor. The obstacles for the development of Capitalist markets are less technical than they are social, cultural and political.

Agrarian Transition

The economic foundations of the feudal agricultural system began to shift substantially in 16th Century England with the breakdown of the manorial system. Instead of a serf-based system of labor, workers were increasingly employed as part of a broader and expanding money-based economy. That system put pressure on both landlords and tenants to increase the productivity and profitability of agriculture. The weakened coercive power of the aristocracy to extract peasant surpluses encouraged them to try better methods. Tenants had incentive to improve their production methods in order to flourish in a competitive labor market.

By the early 17th Century, England was a centralized state from which much of the feudal order of Medieval Europe had been swept away. This centralization was strengthened by a good system of roads and by a disproportionately large capital city, London. The capital acted as a central market hub for the entire country, in striking contrast to the fragmented feudal holdings that prevailed on most parts of European Continent.

Mercantilism

The economic doctrine which appeared during the Enlightenment is commonly called Mercantilism. Its initial period, during the Age of Discovery (1500-1800), was associated with the geographic exploration of foreign lands by merchant traders, especially from England and the Low Countries. Mercantilism was a system of trade for profit, although commodities were still largely produced by non-Capitalist methods. Most scholars consider the era of merchant Capitalism and Mercantilism as the origin of modern Capitalism.

England began a large-scale and integrative approach to Mercantilism during the Elizabethan Era (1558–1603). A systematic and coherent explanation of balance of trade was made public through Thomas Mun's (1571-1641), argument that the balance of foreign trade was the key to a nation's wealth. European merchants, backed by state controls, subsidies and monopolies, made most of their profits by buying and selling goods.

Industrial Capitalism

During the Industrial Revolution of the late 18th Century, industrialists replaced merchants as a dominant factor in the

Capitalist system and affected the decline of the traditional handicraft skills of artisans, guilds and journeymen. During this period, the surplus generated by the rise of commercial agriculture encouraged increased mechanization. Industrial Capitalism marked the development of the factory system of manufacturing, characterized by a complex division of labor between and within work processes and the routines of work tasks.

The Enlightenment, and the forces it unleashed, combined to transform America into an enlightened society for its people. Its philosophy and momentum would dominate until the late 20th Century, when Postmodern skepticism would help foster Tribalism and call into question the American character.

POINTS TO REMEMBER:

- The Enlightenment unlocked human society from domination by church and state and recognized the individual as central to human society;

- It pulled science out of philosophy, allowing technology to expand human knowledge

- It replaced group emphasis with emphasis on the individual as the prime mover in human society

- The Enlightenment created a new system of Capitalism around businesses created by individuals and market freedom.

- The Enlightenment ushered in a new view of human rights and led to new government forms, giving people increased power over their destiny.

- It promoted Capitalism, which became the modern economic engine of society.

CHAPTER FOUR

THE COUNTER ENLIGHTENMENT

The Enlightenment was a dangerous attempt to idolize the untrustworthy individual, use him to replace God with science, and create governments of inequality. **Unknown**

The Counter-Enlightenment was a direct attack against the goals, activities, and accomplishments of the Enlightenment Project. Beginning before the French Revolution (c. 1789), both church and crown, feeling their traditions were threatened by something new, attacked the validity of the Enlightenment. Ultimately, these attacks were not able to overcome the consensus that the Enlightenment was a sound master plan for Western society, so it continued to move forward. Attacks on the Enlightenment returned in the second half of the 20th Century, helping to produce a new Postmodernist view of the world, and setting the stage for American Tribalism.

From a philosophical perspective, the Enlightenment caused an earthquake. The development of the scientific method and its practical applications ripped science from the domain of philosophical contemplation. The work of Descartes and others identified the mind body dichotomy which made reason a threat to religion and to the belief in God. These changes did not sit well with the church, which perceived its power base would be threatened if it could not discredit the new way of thinking.

Resistance to the Enlightenment also came from Conservative political types who were uncomfortable with the number of changes taking place in European society. It disrupted the seats of power and threatened the safety of those dependent on existing institutions. The Enlightenment Age was truly a tribal period because the tribes of new religion and new government were in opposition to those existing previously.

Enlightenment France

A new type of intellectual developed in France during the early part of the 18th Century. Called *Philosophes* (the French word for philosopher), these individuals were atypical truth-seekers who applied the Enlightenment philosophy to history, science, politics, and social issues. Although *Philosophe* is a French word, adherents to its point of view emerged around the world. They considered themselves part of a grand "republic of letters" that transcended national political boundaries.

In France, conflicts developed between the Philosophes and state and religious authorities, and the traditionalists were unable to prevent the new intellectuals from gaining the support of important members of the government. Philosophes used reason to attack superstition, bigotry, and religious fanaticism, which they considered the chief obstacles to free thought and social reform. Voltaire took religious fanaticism as his chief target, commenting that a philosophical spirit is the only thing that can cure a fanatical point of view.

French Enlightenment writers did not oppose organized religion, but they strongly attacked religious intolerance.

They believed a society based on reason would change the way people thought about science and the social problems of their society. The Philosophes believed the spread of knowledge would encourage reform in every aspect of life, from the grain trade to the penal system. Chief among their objectives was intellectual freedom… the freedom to use one's own reason and make public the results. The Philosophes wanted freedom of the press and freedom of religion; they considered those as rights guaranteed by **natural law**. In their view, human progress depended on these freedoms.

In France, opposition to the Philosophes reached a peak in the middle of the 18th Century as cultural institutions and centers of political power applied maximum pressure. The main objective of those opponents was to curtail the flow of illicit, Enlightenment-oriented books. In 1755, the church's national assembly debated the problem of "contagion" spreading throughout the country from the poisonous writings of the Philosophes. Faculty at the Sorbonne issued a steady stream of refutations denouncing the Philosophes' efforts to destroy religion and undermine the authority of kings. Government attention to the number of new books expressing Enlightenment tenets and ideas caused them to proliferate widely. In 1785, the national assembly of the church was forced to admit that the new philosophe is "resounding even in the workshops of the artisan and under the humble roof of peasants".[6] Meanwhile, newspapers, magazines, and plays ridiculed the Philosophes, but without effect.

The work of the Philosophes was an important contribution to the French Revolution. It was attractive to a population which saw their government as an anachronism. The French government's inability to provide affordable grain and prevent starvation was the strongest evidence of their failure. What the traditionalists in France could not do to slow the momentum of the Enlightenment, the Revolution accomplished on their behalf. The French people had succeeded in throwing off the corrupt institutions that held power before the Revolution, but there remained a question of whether the cost was worth it. The upheaval and carnage were horrific and took decades to repair. The desire for change was present in the French people, but there was no

---

[6] Darrin M McMahon. *Enemies of the Enlightenment: The French Counter-Enlightenment and the Making of Modernity.* (Oxford: Oxford University Press. 2001), p. 21.

leadership that could carry the country forward, and little willingness to unify the state among those with their own agendas.

It took until the tenth year of the revolution, when Napoleon Bonaparte seized absolute power, for the French nation to heal and begin to chart its way forward. Enlightenment thinking, wrongly or rightly, was implicated as the cause of tens of thousands of deaths. Napoleon had to walk a fine line between support of and antipathy toward the Enlightenment Project. As the successor to the revolution, he had to broadly embrace it or delegitimize all he had accomplished. He wanted to be the hero who would stabilize French society, so he restored some of the old traditions. He also relaxed sanctions against the Catholic Church allowing it to freely operate again.

Germany

During the period 1780-1815, Anglo-American and German cultures split decisively over the benefits of the Enlightenment. While the United States and England continued to embrace individual freedom and science as the path forward, the Germans moved in the opposite direction. They were troubled by the Enlightenment's implications for religion, morality, and politics. They worried the Enlightenment would undermine their traditional view of God the loving Father and replace it with a view of God as the Supreme Mathematician. The Germans also worried that reason would corrode faith and replace it with a depersonalized logic. They believed science would destroy the human spirit, which depended on freedom to explore and understand the world. If the center of the world was the individual, what would happen to the community? What would happen to the sacrifices human beings made that connected them together? To the Germans, the Enlightenment could only produce a world of cold, selfish people.

Britain

Although Britain was one of the leaders of the Enlightenment, one of its sons, Edmund Burke (1730-1797), was an outspoken critic of the movement. A Catholic, Burke believed that the authority of tradition lay in Christian practice. He held all forms of egalitarianism thinking in contempt because they were incompatible with history and nature. The idea that a human society could create a social world from scratch, as the French tried to do, was abhorrent to him. His theory was later validated when the French Revolution turned bloody.

Burke's criticism of the Enlightenment was essentially political. He believed traditional institutions were imperfect and contained evil, but there was no reason to believe replacing them would lead to a better outcome. Burke believed it was dangerous to give the people too much power and saw his role in Parliament as a platform to block the bad ideas of the majority. Even though Burke was opposed to the French Revolution, he was willing to support revolutions in the right circumstances; the Glorious Revolution of 1688 and the American Revolution being examples. Burke's view was built on Christian faith which was a stronger foundation than the delicate rights and liberties of modern government. He saw the latter as constantly under attack by those who would like to create social improvements.

The Romantic Movement
The Romantic Movement, which occurred between 1800-1850, was another rejection of the Enlightenment Project. Romanticism had its greatest impact in the arts (music, drama, and literature), but it also had an intellectual focus. The movement reacted against the determinism and structure

of the Enlightenment and it's offspring, the Industrial Revolution. The Enlightenment created a structured world featuring equations instead of emotions, which the Romantics saw as unacceptable.

Romanticism emphasized emotion, individualism, and the glorification of the past. Intense emotion was an authentic source of aesthetic experience; there was new emphasis on apprehension, horror, terror, and awe, especially as experienced in confronting the aesthetic beauty of nature. Folk art and ancient customs were noble and worthy of celebration; spontaneity was a desirable characteristic. In contrast to the Rationalism and Classicism of the Enlightenment, Romanticism revived elements of art perceived as authentically Medieval, setting it apart from urban sprawl and industrialism.

Although Romanticism was rooted in the German *sturm und drang* (storm and stress) literary movement, which preferred intuition and emotion over the rationalism of the Enlightenment, the events and ideologies of the French Revolution were also important. Romanticism glorified the achievements of "heroic" individualists and artists, maintaining their examples would raise the quality of society. It also promoted the individual imagination as a critical authority, allowing it to be free from the constraints of classical notions of form in art. There was a strong attraction to historical and natural inevitability, a *zeitgeist*, that described the spirit of the times. Not essential to Romanticism, but widespread enough to be part of it, was a strong belief and interest in nature. This particularly focused on the effects of nature upon the artist when it surrounded him. In contrast to the social art of the Enlightenment, Romantics were distrustful of the human world, and believed instead that a close connection with nature was mentally and morally healthy. Romantic art was created to speak to its audiences using the personal voice of the artist. In literature, romantic poetry invited the reader to identify the protagonists with the poets themselves.

According to Isaiah Berlin, Romanticism embodied

a new and restless spirit, seeking violently to burst through old and cramping forms, a nervous preoccupation with perpetually changing inner states of consciousness, a longing for the unbounded and the indefinable, for perpetual movement and change, an effort to return to the forgotten sources of life, a passionate effort at self-assertion both individual and collective, a search after means of expressing an unappeasable yearning for unattainable goals.[7]

The Romantics relationship to the French Revolution, in the very early stages of the period, was clearly important, but highly variable, depending on geography and individual reactions. Most Romantics could be regarded as broadly progressive in their views, but a considerable number always had, or developed, a wide range of conservative views. One of Romanticism's key ideas and most enduring legacies has been the assertion of nationalism, which became a central theme of Romantic art and political philosophy.

Philosophy turns against the Enlightenment

In philosophy, Rationalism is the view that reason is the chief source and test of knowledge. Rationalists argued that certain truths existed and that the intellect can directly grasp these truths. They also believed that certain rational principles existed in logic, mathematics, ethics, and

---

[7] Isaiah Berlin. 1990. *The Crooked Timber of Humanity: Chapters in the History of Ideas.* (Ed. Henry Hardy, London: John Murray, 199), p. 96.

metaphysics. These principles were so fundamentally true that denying them would cause one to fall into contradiction. The Rationalists had such high confidence in reason that empirical proof and physical evidence were regarded as unnecessary to ascertain certain truths. In other words, there were significant ways to gain knowledge independently of sense experience.

This Enlightenment's confidence in reason was called into question by Hume and others who pointed out the unreliability of data observed or received through the senses. One person's view of the world was never identical to another person's view, so there could be no absolute truth. Hume's ideology had two major impacts on philosophy during the Enlightenment period. The first was on science, which was entirely dependent on empirical data to prove its theories and accurately explain how the world operated. Hume forced science to redefine itself and prove that the results of experimentation were reliable.

In the 19th Century, a theoretical response to Hume appeared in the work of Charles Sanders Peirce (1839-1914), an American philosopher and statistician. Peirce created the term "fallibilism" to explain how science could successfully deal with the problem of misperception of experimental data. Fallibilism asserted that no belief had a justification sufficient or robust enough to guarantee the truth of that belief. That means science could only be trusted as reliable if it agreed that knowledge did not require certainty. The scientific method left the truth of any experiment open to the chance that some future experiment would show it to be false. This uncertainty would lead to the creation of alternative hypotheses and further data gathering. That new data would either support or contradict what was assumed to be the truth.

The second major impact of Hume was his philosophical view on perception and knowledge. In the two centuries since Hume's time, philosophy has grappled with what is knowable with certainty; arguments for and against absolute knowledge reached a dead end in the 1960s. This skepticism about truth was a factor in the acceptance of Postmodernism which espoused its own definition of truth.

Kant and his successors
Kant's view of knowledge assumed that reality was barred to reason and was limited to awareness and understanding of its own subjective products. For reason to be objective, it

must have contact with reality. If the senses gave us only internal representations of objects, there was an obstacle that existed between reality and reason, making reality subjective. This notion of the limits to our understanding of the world had a profound impact on all philosophy after Kant. Those who followed him had to unravel the new world he created. Out of these efforts, three schools of thought emerged: one ignored the problem of perception and knowledge; one embraced irrationality as a substitute; and the other reduced reality to logic.

Ignoring the problems of perception

Georg Wilhelm Friedrich Hegel (1770-1831), ignored philosophical problems with the external world and built a philosophical system around being. He refused to accept Hume's limitations on what was knowable, declaring that even if one accepts the subjectivity of reality, it doesn't matter, because the constructed perception is the reality for that person. The subject of a perception was real and so the external world was the sum of the perceptions built by that individual. Hegel's concept of reason was based on a constructive process and not a perception. If that process was followed correctly, truth would follow regardless of perception.

Irrationalism from Kierkegaard and Nietzsche

Competition to Hegel's ideas emerged from the Irrationalist wing of German philosophy. These Irrationalists were divided over religion: Fredrich Schleiermacher (1768-1834), and Soren Kierkegaard (1813-1855), were theists; Arthur Schopenhauer (1788-1860), and Fredrich Nietzsche (1844-1900), were atheists. All harbored contempt for reason and looked for better ways to understand reality. Like the Romantics they decided that understanding must come through faith, emotions, and instinct.

Schleiermacher asserted that religious feelings were similar to perception and provided man with access to an alternate reality. Those feelings could only be directed inward. The nature of religion, according to Schleiermacher, was the feeling of dependence on God. Reason was corrupt because it provided independence instead of dependence. Kierkegaard, also a Christian, asserted that accepting one's religious beliefs required an irrational leap of faith that could not be explained by logic or reason.

Schopenhauer fought against the value of religion as an outcome of attacks on reason. Reason's characteristics did not fit a reality that was its opposite. Once a man understood the cruel nature of life, he must be skeptical about the future. Nietzsche believed one must be true to oneself and break out of the artificial structure of reason, because reason was a tool for weaklings. The enlightened man of the future would not play category games to avoid conflict. He would move forward by embracing conflict, utilizing his senses and natural emotions to live the truest life.

By the turn of the 20th Century, philosophy stood at a crossroads. The tired arguments over the accuracy of knowledge gave way to more concrete approaches to solving philosophical problems. New philosophical ideas would emerge that were opposed to the Enlightenment's optimistic view of knowledge and reason.

The Postmodernists represented the culmination of the Counter-Enlightenment. The story they had to tell seemed to describe a postmodern world. That story was attractive to those who were crying out for an ideological foundation that could explain a fragmented, fast-paced world. Postmodernism, however, also represented and endorsed social fragmentation, which took America farther down the road to Tribalism.

POINTS TO REMEMBER

- The Counter-Enlightenment was a historical movement opposed to the Enlightenment Project.

- Initial resistance was strongest in Germany and France and weaker in England and the United States.

- The Romantic Movement was a direct reaction against the Enlightenment and saw it as too deterministic and structured, thereby destroying the beauty of the world.

- Counter-Enlightenment thinkers attacked science and forced it to redefine its approach to allow for fallibility.

- Counter-Enlightenment thinking led philosophy down a path of analyzing being and perception in ways that were critical of the Enlightenment's belief in reason.

- In the 1970s, the attack on the Enlightenment became a founding principle of the Postmodernist Movement.

CHAPTER FIVE

THE MODERN AGE

Modernity exists in the form of a desire to wipe out whatever came earlier, in the hope of reaching at least a point that could be called a true present, a point of origin that marks a new departure. **Paul de Man**

Most people associate the word "Modern" with the 1950s and 1960s, the period after World War II when prosperity was widespread in the United States. New homes sprouted up in the suburbs and featured the latest time-saving appliances. Television sets became part of the furniture; automobiles became available to almost every American;

and people traveled the interstate highways on vacation. It was a time of leisurely suburban living.

The truth is the Modern Age began with the Renaissance in the late 16th Century. The term "modern" was invented at that time to indicate "present" or "recent" times. It comes from the Latin adverb modo, meaning "just now."

The Modern Era is the practical manifestation of the Enlightenment. The Enlightenment created the toolset, including, individualism, capitalism, and science. The Modern Era applied those tools to human society, impacting politics, society and culture in a new effort to utilize reason.

Historians break down the Modern Era into periods: The Early Modern period, which began in the early 16th Century; the Late Modern period, which began in the late 18th Century; and the Contemporary Modern period, which spanned the years from 1945 to the present day.

In the pre-Modern era, the human sense of self and purpose were most often expressed via a faith in God. At the same time, there was no focus on individuality or any role for the individual outside of a group. Religious authorities, from their positions of power, were the spiritual intermediaries between God and the common man, and the masses had access to God only through those intermediaries. From the time man could first contemplate his existence, faith and religious tradition were a sacred part of the human belief system.

Early Modern Period

Although the starting and ending points are open to debate, the timeframe of the Early Modern Period roughly spans the decades from 1500 through the time of the French Revolution, starting in 1789. One could further define its onset with the Fall of Constantinople in 1453, the Renaissance period, or the Age of Discovery.

Historians in recent decades have argued that the most important feature of the Early Modern period was its focus on globalization. The period witnessed the exploration and colonization of the Americas and the rise of sustained contacts between previously isolated parts of the globe. European powers became involved in global trade; the exchange of goods, plants, animals, and food crops were extended to the New World. New economies and institutions emerged and became more sophisticated and globally articulated over the course of the period. This process began in the medieval North Italian city-states, particularly Genoa, Venice, and Milan. The Early Modern period also included the rise of the dominance of the economic theory of mercantilism, the European colonization of the Americas, Asia, and Africa, and the spread of Christianity around the world.

Early Modern trends in various regions of the world represented a shift away from medieval modes of political and economic organization. Feudalism declined in Europe, while the period also included the Protestant Reformation and the disastrous Thirty Years' War. Additional hallmarks of the period included the development of experimental science, accelerated travel due to improvements in mapping and ship design, increasingly rapid technological progress, secularized civic politics, and the emergence of nation states.

Finally, there was the impact of Enlightenment thinking on politics. Man's desire for individual freedom and liberty led directly to the American and French Revolutions, both of which ordained democracy as the new form of government, to replace the old monarchical systems.

Late Modern Period

The Industrial Revolutions were major technological, socioeconomic, and cultural changes in late 18th and early 19th Centuries that began in Britain and spread throughout the world. The impact of this change on society was enormous and was often compared to the Neolithic revolution, when mankind developed agriculture and gave up his nomadic lifestyle. Along with increased productivity and the enormous expansion of goods available to the public, came severe problems with human working conditions. Reform movements began in response to the negative impact industrial work was having on the lives of employees. The reformists' ideas were grounded in Liberalism, although they also possessed aspects of Utopian, Socialist, and religious ideas. This radical movement campaigned for electoral reform, relief for the poor, free trade, educational reform, prison reform, and public sanitation. Continuous pressure over many decades saw the implementation of many of these initiatives.

In the 1800s and early 1900s, once great and powerful Empires such as Spain, Ottoman Turkey, the Mughal Empire, and the Kingdom of Portugal began to break apart. The decline of Spain, which had been a leading power in

Europe for five hundred years, was accelerated by the invasion of Napoleon Bonaparte. Sensing the time was right, Spain's vast colonies in South America began a series of rebellions that ended with most of the Spanish territories gaining their independence.

Slavery was greatly reduced around the world in the 19th Century. Following a successful slave revolt in Haiti, Britain forced the Barbary pirates to halt their practice of kidnapping and enslaving Europeans, banned slavery throughout its domain, and charged its navy with ending the global slave trade. Later, slavery was abolished in Russia, America, and Brazil.

Charles Darwin introduced the theory of evolution to the world in 1859, using the example of finches in the Galapagos Islands as evidence for a genetic link between species. Darwin's theories had an enormous impact on man's perception of the history of the world and his place in it. The Enlightenment's spiritual philosophy was developed from earlier secular traditions and carried through most of the modern period. Humanist ethical philosophies affirmed the dignity and worth of all people, based on the ability to determine right and wrong. This was an appeal to universal human qualities, particularly rationality, and avoidance of the supernatural or alleged divine authority from religious texts.

Modern political theory was advanced by Karl Marx (1818-1883), one of the founders of sociology and the person who most strongly advocated a collectivist view of society. Marx asserted that the Capitalist economic system would foster a low-end worker class that would eventually revolt against their exploitation at the hands of business owners. The outcome of the revolt would be a new society, based on government ownership of the means of production. That society would destroy economic classes and create equality for all citizens. Marx' influence was enormous and has carried forward to the current day.

The Late Modern Period ended with the two world wars: the first from 1914-1918 and the second from 1939-1945. During the First World War, the Russian Revolution took place and resulted in the creation of the first Communist nation in the world. The rise of Fascism did not represent the coming of a new right-wing ideology, it was a modern form of collectivist Socialism. It competed directly with the Communist ideology and was the system of choice by the people of Germany. Unfortunately, the Germans did not foresee the megalomania of Adolf Hitler, which would nearly destroy their nation.

The genocide of World War II appalled the world, putting a stain forever on collectivist authoritarian models of government. The idea of building a similar model, in the future, was abhorrent to all except a few extremists. The Communist model was also a failure during this period. Living on borrowed time, the Soviet Union set itself up as the nuclear adversary of the United States and this conflict launched the Cold War period.

The Late Modern Period in the United States
In the United States, the fifty years before the Civil War, saw increasing division, based on the growth of slavery in the American South and in the Western territories. The period was also significant because it marked the transition of American manufacturing to a mass production economy. The American Civil War began when the Southern slave states declared their secession from the United States and formed the Confederate States of America. Led by Jefferson Davis, they fought against the United States government

under President Abraham Lincoln, who was supported by all the free states in the North.

Following the Civil War, the Gilded Age (1870-1900), produced substantial growth in population in the United States along with extravagant displays of wealth and excess by America's upper-class. The businessmen of this Second Industrial Revolution created industrial towns and cities in the Northeast and cities with new factories, and that contributed to the creation of an ethnically diverse industrial working class. Exploitation of the working class generated the wealth of the rising super-rich industrialists and financiers called "robber barons." One prominent example was John D. Rockefeller, who was an important figure in shaping the new oil industry. He used highly effective tactics and aggressive business practices to absorb or destroy most of his competition.

The Gilded Age was another era of Tribalism in the United States, driven by the same forces that formed the political parties and fought the Civil War. The rich were exploiting the poor who had no recourse to protect themselves. The blatant immorality was egregious enough to produce an activist faction in opposition to the perpetrators. The federal government responded to demands for reform by passing new laws that offered basic protection for workers. It was the young Progressive Movement that acted as prime mover for these changes.

The creation of a modern industrial economy took place during this same period. Once the construction of a transportation and communication infrastructure was complete, the corporation became the dominant form of business organization. Its human representative, the business manager, transformed business operations through a focus on efficiency. In response to a perceived dangerous growth in corporate power, Congress passed the Sherman Antitrust Act, the first of the American anti-monopoly laws. On paper, this law forbade every contract, scheme, deal, or conspiracy to restrain trade, leaving the definition of "restraint" as subjective and situational.

By the beginning of the 20th Century, per capita income and industrial production in the United States exceeded those of any other country, except Britain. Long hours and hazardous working conditions drove workers to form labor unions despite strong opposition from industrialists and the courts. Following a period of prosperity, two world wars and the

Great Depression caused a great disruption to the United States economy and the harm to the American people. This instability was not resolved until the end of World War II.

The Contemporary Modern Period in the United States
Starting in 1945, the United States entered a long era of social, economic, and cultural change. The next three decades would include the country's greatest period of prosperity based on improved productivity and the introduction of new technologies that became available to most Americans. Radical, social and cultural changes followed the idealistic period of the 1950s, proving that the calmness of the 1950s was a false reality.

The South saw the biggest socio-economic change of any region, during this period; a transition from an agricultural region to a business-oriented industrial region began. Meanwhile, two significant African-American migrations occurred at this time. One from South to North prior to the mid-1970s and then a reverse migration, starting in the late 1970s. The northern migration was driven by a desire to escape racism and find better jobs; the reverse migration was driven by economic decline in the North and the improvement in economic conditions in the South.

In the remainder of the country, the big change was in residential living patterns. The combination of a postwar housing boom and the VA loan program stimulated suburban housing production and moved families to the edges of cities.

The Cold War

The Cold War began in the mid-1940s and lasted into the early 1990s. Throughout this period, the ideological conflict between East and West was expressed through military coalitions, espionage, weapons development, propaganda, and competitive technological development. It also generated costly defense spending, a massive conventional and nuclear arms race, and numerous proxy wars. Fortunately for the world, the two superpowers never came to the point of fighting each other directly.

The Soviet Union created the Eastern Bloc of countries, annexing some as Soviet Socialist Republics and maintaining others as satellite states that would later form the Warsaw Pact. The United States and various Western European countries began a policy of containment of Communism and forged alliances, including NATO, for this purpose. Several of the Western European countries coordinated efforts to rebuild Western Europe, including West Germany, which the Soviets opposed. In other regions of the world, such as Latin America and Southeast Asia, the Soviet Union fostered Communist revolutionary movements, which the United States and many of its allies opposed and attempted to roll back.

Consumerism

As the 1950s began, the average American enjoyed an income more than fifteen times greater than that of the average foreigner. The period of industrial growth following the end of World War II included a refocusing on consumer goods. Americans were caught up in a lifestyle of shopping and consumption. General Motors benefited greatly from the postwar economic boom and, as the symbol for American industrialism, had a massive influence on the preferences and tastes of consumers. Americans were encouraged to trade in their cars every year for bigger, newer, and better models. Failing to do so was considered un-American.

The American Dream was now owning a new home. Americans felt the pull of suburbia and began to migrate from cities into surrounding rural areas, creating a demand for more shopping facilities, restaurants, schools, churches and recreational facilities in the suburbs. Shopping and buying became major American pastimes as the ripple effect of the new affluence started to permeate throughout the economy. The McDonald brothers invented a new way for Americans to eat, making food faster, cheaper, and more consistent. Ray Kroc built an empire using their model.

In the Fifties, men were expected to be the eager breadwinners, while women were told to be devoted homemakers. For women, housekeeping and raising a family were considered ideal female roles. Companies advertised housekeeping items for women and children began to see ads directed to them.

Mass media

Television was poised to dominate the media industry in 1950. There were 3.1 million television sets in American homes, and over 100 television stations operating in 38 states across the USA that year. This period has been called the Golden Age of Television. Cinema, radio and print media were its major competitors, but television gave Americans the best of both worlds: pictures and sound, in the comfort of their living rooms. With the growing popularity of television, print media, radio and film were forced to rethink their approaches towards news and entertainment.

Television became a hot advertising medium in the 1950s; television advertisements projected fantasies about products and how they could make people happy and successful. Commercials were carefully packaged to influence the viewer and companies sponsored specific television programs to get their name in front of the public. Some unethical advertisers used dishonest means to raise viewership rates for the shows they sponsored. When it was discovered that some of the most popular quiz shows, including the famous "$64,000 Question" and "Twenty-One," had been rigged to make them more exciting, the news of cheating prompted a negative reaction from the public.

In 1952, Dwight Eisenhower used television advertising in a presidential campaign for the first time. Soon, all presidential candidates would rely on television advertising to communicate their positions to the masses.

Civil Rights Movement
The Civil Rights Movement began with the goal of ending racial segregation and discrimination against African

Americans and securing legal recognition of their citizenship rights, as enumerated in the Constitution. The most popular strategies designed to achieve this outcome were based on the notion of non-violent civil disobedience and included such methods of protest as boycotts, freedom rides, voter registration drives, sit-ins, and marches. A series of critical rulings and laws, from the 1954 Brown v. Board of Education to the Civil Rights Acts of 1964 and Voting Rights Act of 1965, outlawed major forms of discrimination against African Americans and women, including racial segregation and unequal application of voter registration requirements. A wave of inner-city riots in black communities from 1964 through 1970 undercut support from the white community.

The emerging Black Power movement, which lasted from about 1966 to 1975, demanded political and economic self-sufficiency for African Americans. During the March Against Fear in 1966, the Student Nonviolent Coordinating Committee and Congress of Racial Equality fully embraced the slogan of Black Power that described a trend toward militancy and self-reliance

New Wave of Feminism

In contrast to earlier women's movements, the Second Wave of Feminism broadened the debate of women's rights to encompass a wider range of issues, including sexuality, reproductive rights, family, the workplace, and legal and economic inequalities. Just as the abolitionist movement made 19th Century women more aware of their lack of power, the protest movements of the 1960s inspired many white and middle-class women to create their own movement with the goal of seeking broader rights.

Betty Friedan 's book *The Feminine Mystique*, disputed the post-World War II expectation of women as suburban housewives. Friedan and others radically changed the face of Western culture, leading to marital rape laws, the establishment of rape crisis and battered women's shelters, significant changes in custody and divorce law, modifications to credit and ownership, and widespread integration of women into sports activities and in the workplace. Following legislative victories in the early 1960s, Friedan joined with others to create the National Organization for Women (NOW), which advocated for full rights to women.

Sexual Revolution

Following World War II, and during the "baby boom" (1946-1964), the birth control movement reached its goal of making birth control legal. Its advocacy for reproductive rights transitioned into a new era that focused on abortion, public funding, and insurance coverage. Birth control was officially legalized following the Supreme Court ruling in Griswold v. Connecticut in 1965, while the Roe v. Wade decision in 1973 legalized abortion during the first trimester of pregnancy.

Use of oral contraceptives spread rapidly during the latter part of the 1960s. "The Pill" was endorsed and distributed by doctors as part of President Johnson's social reform policy. Fear of global overpopulation became a major issue in the 1960s, generating concerns about pollution, food shortages, and quality of life, and leading to well-funded birth control campaigns around the world. The ability of women to control fertility produced a sharp increase in college attendance and graduation rates for women.

The New Left

In the United States, the "New Left" was the name associated with Liberal, sometimes radical, political movements that appeared during the 1960s, primarily among college students. The New Left was a loosely organized, mostly white student movement that protested the Vietnam War and advocated for democracy, civil rights, and various types of university reforms.

It opposed what it saw as the prevailing authority structures in society, which it termed "the Establishment." Those who rejected this authority became known as "anti-Establishment." The New Left drew inspiration from black radicalism, particularly the Black Power movement and the left-wing Black Panther Party. It did not seek to recruit industrial workers, but concentrated on a social activist approach to organizing, convinced they could be the source for a more effective social revolution. The New Left was also a player in the modern environmentalist movement, which clashed with the Old Left's support of union jobs over concerns about the environment.

The Environment

The Environmental Movement in the United States arose from the activist conservationist efforts of John Muir, founder of the Sierra Club, and was rooted in early 20th Century efforts to protect natural resources. The movement grew in the 1960s with a focus on wildlife preservation, air and water pollution, global population control, and preventing the exploitation of natural resources. Using direct action, lobbying, and research to achieve its environmental goals, Greenpeace established itself by protesting underground nuclear weapons testing in the late 1960s. Global awareness of environmentalism led to the creation of international events to increase awareness, such as Earth Day and the United Nations Conference on the Human Environment. The passage of the Clean Air Act and Clean Water Act during the 1970s came as a result of an increasing focus on the environment as a top tier issue.

Gay Rights

Gay and lesbian rights movements developed in the post-World War II years, and sought social acceptance and equality for lesbian, gay, bisexual, transgender, and queer (LGBTQ) people. The early "homophile" movement differed from the Gay Rights Movement of the 1960s, because the former focused on non-confrontation and assimilation, while the later took a more radical approach and sought public acceptance. The New York Stonewall Riots in June of 1969 were a series of uprisings and resistance against a violent police raid on the Stonewall Inn, which openly welcomed gay people and catered to the most marginalized people in the community.

Gays agitated to overturn state laws which strictly prohibited their lifestyle; laws in place since the founding of the Republic. Those laws began to be repealed in 1962, but it wasn't until 2003 that the last one of them was overturned.

Reaction Against the Modern World

Starting in the late 1970s, the United States and Western Europe saw a public reaction against the commercial corruption of their societies. Consumerism was labeled decadent and wasteful, because it left legions of people in poverty. The Viet Nam War had shown the corruption of the Military-Industrial Complex and its association with the power-hungry political elites.

From a sociological standpoint, popular culture became a tremendous influence; ubiquitous but also superficial and dynamic, changing from day to day.

Western democracies appeared to be at a crossroads, unable to accommodate special interest groups' demands for new rights. The Cold War droned on with its larger and larger stockpiles of nuclear weapons. Feminists, homosexuals, and African-Americans were agitating to have more control over their lives. Changes were happening faster than society could adapt to them. The result was a high level of public dissatisfaction. A debate about whether the Modern Era had ended began in earnest. Intellectuals were asking themselves, "If Modernism is dead, how could the Western World move into the future without a link to its past?"

Tribalism Emerges

The tribes in late 20th Century America were now formed. On the Left, were those who viewed the changes to society as a signal to move in a different direction. Their plan included the teardown of the Modern Age. On the Right, there was a tightening of the Conservative view. Increasing uncertainty strengthened their effort to resist change.

POINTS TO REMEMBER

- The word "modern" implies recent times, but actually refers to Western history after 1500.

- The Early Modern period (1500-1789), covers the time from the transition of Europe away from medieval institutions to the French Revolution (1789). This included new political ideas, the development of economic principles, the expansion of the role of science, and the globalization of trade.

- The late Modern period (1789-1945), was a time of enormous change. Industrialization and mass production increased the availability of goods to all mankind. Human rights improved with the abolition of slavery. Darwin introduced his concept of evolution. Marx developed his model of Socialism.

- Contemporary modern history began at the end of World War II and encompasses enormous changes in Western society.

- The Cold War and economic prosperity were hallmarks of the 1950s, while the 1960s witnessed great upheaval over Civil Rights and the Viet Nam war.

- Starting in the 1970s, new technology, mass media, consumerism, and increased communications changed the lives of Americans forever.

- These changes were enormously disruptive and stimulated the rise of new social movements. Second Wave Feminism, the sexual revolution, the environment, and gay rights were all changing the character of American culture.

CHAPTER SIX

THE HISTORY OF COLLECTIVISM

Collectivism and freedom are mortal enemies. Only one will survive.

G. Edward Griffin

The story of Collectivism is the story of opposition to the Enlightenment. Although labeled a Counter-Enlightenment concept, Collectivism was not based on resistance. Instead, it emerged from forces competing with and intending to replace the old European political order with something better. One could suggest that Collectivists were tribal, sharing a common belief system, but there was no opposing tribe. The strength and power of Individualism during the Enlightenment dominated but it took the Collectivists one hundred years to form a significant opposition. There was, however, a battle waged between Individualists and Collectivists in the field of philosophy. Some, like Kant and Hegel, were Collectivists; others, like Locke, believed in the individual. Collectivists fought for their cause for two centuries, until their dreams proved impractical. Eventually, Collectivists rode the horses of identity politics and Postmodernism to seriously challenge the individualism of the Enlightenment.

Collectivism was a philosophical idea that placed human groups above individuals in a culture or society. Group thinking was all encompassing and cohesive, so it offered greater benefits to society, according to its adherents. Collectivist thinking had been a part of the European social fabric since Rousseau, who believed that mankind had become corrupted by the individualism of the Enlightenment.

After Rousseau, Collectivism took parallel paths. One was developed in Germany and would later become the intellectual foundation for Hitler and Nazism. That was a right-wing version based on authoritarian control. The economic version, labeled Socialism, developed as a left-wing ideology. Collectivist thinking today is supported by the political left and remains a counter ideology to Capitalism among those who refuse to accept Capitalism's inherent inequality. Right-wing Collectivism was discredited by the excess of the Nazis, although fringe groups still support its ideas.

Rousseau's Collectivism

Rousseau believed that civilization developed at the expense of morality. The root of moral degradation was reason, as defined by the Enlightenment. Before they were able to reason, human beings lived simple lives. As time went on, man's behavior led to a surplus of wealth and claims of property rights. Property ownership motivated men to accumulate wealth at the expense of the less fortunate. Moreover, having succeeded in the competition of life, the rich fought to protect their positions and possessions, which expanded the inequality between them and the poor. Rousseau sought the creation of a new society that would stand in the middle ground between the idle rich and a primitive state. This new state would be governed by religion which would act as a stabilizing force. Reason was destructive to society; natural passion must replace it. This became manifest with the French Revolution which, during its constitutional phase, followed the ideas of Rousseau.

Collectivist thinking emerged on both the Left and Right after Rousseau. These natural opponents were linked by the desire to oppose the Enlightenment, to advocate for strong government, support state religion, show disinterest toward science, and express strong rejection of violence. For all the differences between Left and Right, their common enemy was Individualism which had cursed the West with Capitalism, limited government, separation of church and state, and economic optimism.

Collectivism in Germany

To the Germans, the killing of the French King (Louis XVI), was appalling. When they were later defeated by Napoleon, the Germans concluded that the Enlightenment was corrupt and disastrous for mankind. Immanuel Kant (1724-1804), would react to the times and chart a new philosophical path for the German people.

Separate from his theory of knowledge, which was anti-reason, Kant lectured on and wrote about many subjects, including physics, anthropology, meteorology, psychology, and history. His advocacy of the Enlightenment appeared in his paper *What is Enlightenment?* Kant called out the laziness of mankind and man's willingness to let others block his ability to reason. The key to human Enlightenment was freedom, so if a society could be constructed that allowed men to use reason in all matters, mankind could move toward enlightenment. This objective could not be accomplished quickly because it needed to be implemented carefully.

In contrast to positions that were foundational to the Enlightenment, Kant was an advocate of Collectivism and war. In his paper, *An Idea for a Universal History with a Cosmopolitan Aim,* Kant defined mankind as a collective. In nature, Kant asserted, the individual meant nothing. Furthermore, development of the individual conflicted with the development of the species. Nature propelled itself forward mechanically as a machine, reacting to its environment and creating new creatures. Whether or not any one species survives depended on its adaptability.

In his *Idea for Universal History*, Kant stated that war was a useful tool to carry man into the future. One outcome of living in society was man's antagonism toward other men and antagonism often led to war. Besides having a cleansing effect on human society, war was nature's way of bringing forth the higher development of man's capacities. In other words, Kant posited, once the natural antagonism of man against man exhausted itself through war, man could achieve permanent peace. War was appropriate and useful to resolve human conflicts, so the German people had to defeat lesser nations when they stood in the way. Kant's positions contributed to the foundation of the German Collectivist thinking that developed after him.

Herder

Johann Herder (1744-1803), was a German philosopher and literary critic who was formally trained for a career as a clergyman. Between 1764-69, he began publishing essays on literary criticism. In 1770, he met Johann Wolfgang von Goethe (1749-1832), and convinced the great writer to break away from a traditional writing style and create his own.

Intellectually, Herder made his greatest contribution in the study of language. In 1772, he published *A Treatise on the Origin of Language*, which encouraged the German people to embrace their own languages and dialects, rather than adapt to those of other cultures. Herder was one of the first to argue that language contributed to shaping the frameworks and the patterns with which each linguistic community thought and felt. For Herder, language was "the organ of thought," it was both the means and the expression of man's creative capacity and his ability to communicate with others. In this sense, Herder argued that all thinking was thinking in language.

By 1776, Herder had shifted his philosophy towards a more classical approach. He published *Outline of a Philosophical History of Humanity*, which emphasized the historical and physical circumstances of human development. To Herder, one had to be immersed in the age, the geography, and the history of society to understand it fully. At that time, Germany was part of the Holy Roman Empire and was divided into many individual states and kingdoms. Herder pushed for cultural affinity to bring all the German people together into a single culture with a single language.

The world's nations were both individual and separate, distinguished by climate, education, foreign interaction, and heredity. Herder praised Providence for having separated nationalities not only by woods and mountains, seas and deserts, rivers and climates, but more particularly by language and character. Herder praised a tribal outlook (the nation as a tribe) and wrote that the savage who loves his family and accepts his tribe is a better man than the cultivated man who is in love with his species. Furthermore, every nation belonged to its own people, independent of all others. To Herder, the German people were a tribe by nature. He wanted to use that characteristic to turn Germany into a nation-tribe, not a nation of tribes like 21st Century America has become.

Herder saw national glory as a deceptive trap. In the extreme, it dominated the mind and closed it off from competing impressions. He pointed out the danger of cultural superiority which could lead to exploitation of minority groups. He singled out the Jewish people as a culture who should not be abused because they had suffered enough already. History, however, did not honor his position.

Enlightenment thinkers believed that all cultures could move forward together as part of a universal process. This was not possible, according to Herder, because different cultures exist in different forms because of their own unique histories. The notion of combining cultures was dangerous because it produced dilution and decay. For the Germans grafting Enlightenment branches onto their tree would be a disaster. It would be better for them to be rooted in their own identity.

Fichte

Johann Gottlieb Fichte (1762-1814), was a prominent German philosopher best known for creating German Idealism, which he modeled after the philosophy of Kant. His principal concerns were subjectivity and consciousness. His work is relevant here because of his collectivist views on German Nationalism and the need for an approach to education that would solidify the German people. Fichte saw the future of Germany as dependent on a mandatory educational system that was uniform across the country. Students must be indoctrinated in the way Germans must think of themselves. They were a part of a united nation that must be protected from outsiders.

Fichte attended the University of Jena but could not finish because he was unable to pay his tuition. After studying the works of Kant, Fichte sought an interview with him, but Kant refused. Fichte then decided to write an essay, *Attempt at a Critique of All Revelation* to impress Kant. In it, he investigated the connections between divine revelation and Kant's critical philosophy. That essay was published without Fichte's knowledge and without his name on it. Readers came to believe it was written by Kant himself. Kant denied authorship but praised it, and Fichte became an instant celebrity.

Fichte went on to develop a new philosophy of consciousness and perception. He argued that self-consciousness was a social phenomenon, an important step and perhaps the first clear step in this direction by modern philosophy. A necessary condition of every subject's self-awareness was the existence of other rational subjects. Interacting with other individuals brought a person out of their state of unconsciousness and into an awareness of themselves as free individuals.

Between December 1807 and March 1808, Fichte gave a series of lectures concerning the need for a "German Nation" which would embrace one culture and language, and project the kind of national education he hoped would raise up Germany from its humiliating defeat at the hands of the French under Napoleon. As a supporter of Revolutionary France, Fichte became disenchanted by its direction as

Napoleon's armies advanced through Europe, occupying German territories, stripping them of their raw materials and subjugating the German people to French rule. He came to believe that Germany must shoulder the responsibility of carrying the true virtues of the French Revolution, Liberty, Equality, and Fraternity, into the future.

Fichte gave a set of lectures, entitled the *Addresses to the German Nation*, which coincided with a period of reform in the Prussian government, under the chancellorship of Baron Von Stein. They displayed Fichte's interest in language and culture as vehicles of human spiritual development. Fichte built upon the earlier ideas of Herder and attempted to unite them with his own systematic approach. The aim of the German nation, he stated, was to create an empire that would destroy the physical force that ruled the world. Like Herder's German nationalism, Fichte's nationalism was wholly cultural, and grounded in aesthetic, literary, and moral principles.

Fichte believed that the German defeat at the hands of Napoleon was due to a failed educational system. The weakness of the government allowed the neglect of duty to go unpunished. Education, he espoused, had to be equitable and universal. Compulsion, not free will, was best for students. Academics should be a microcosm of what the ideal society should be like; education would eliminate self-interest and advocate the pure love of duty. Education was a link in the eternal chain of human life in a higher social order. If Germany could not reform itself, it would die and take down Europe with it.

Hegel

Hegel liked Rousseau and if Rousseau was correct, the Enlightenment notion of freedom was a fraud. Hegel believed that all human possessions came through the state. Human history consisted of working out what was absolute, whether it was God, universal reason, or the divine idea. The carrying out of God's plan was human history. The state was the instrument of God's plan, so duty to the state was more important than personal interest.

Kant, Herder, Fichte, and Hegel were on the Left politically and the Right ideologically; they were anti-Enlightenment, but not conservative. The European political Left also had another faction, the Socialists, who were developing their own ideology in parallel with other German Collectivist thinkers.

The Beginning of Economic Socialism

Henri de Saint-Simon (1760–1825), the founder of French Socialism, argued that a brotherhood of man must accompany the scientific organization of industry and society. He proposed that the state carry out production and distribution, allowing everyone to have equal opportunity to develop their talents, and this would lead to social harmony. If this could be accomplished, the traditional state could be virtually eliminated, as rule over men was replaced by the administration of society.

Charles Fourier

François Marie Charles Fourier (1772–1837), was a French Utopian Socialist and philosopher who inspired the founding of the Communist community, La Reunion, near present-day Dallas, Texas as well as several other communities within the United States. Fourier's ideas manifested themselves in the middle of the 19th Century when literally hundreds of communes were founded on Fourierist principles in France, North America, Mexico, South America, and Europe. These communities were tribes of shared interest, trying to build a successful collective community. All failed for a variety of reasons; disagreements about administration and climatic conditions being the most common. In reality, shared interest was only an ideal. Practical living could not overcome the psychological, temperamental, and intellectual differences between people which ultimately drove them apart. Forced Tribalism could never emulate the natural Tribalism that had worked so well in nature.

Robert Owen

Robert Owen (1771–1858), advocated the transformation of society into small, local collectives in an attempt to avoid elaborate systems of social organization. Beginning in 1800, he transformed life in the village of New Lanark, Scotland, with ideas and opportunities which were at least a hundred years ahead of their time. Child labor and corporal punishment were abolished; villagers were provided decent homes, schools and evening classes, free health-care, and affordable food.

After leaving England for the United States, Owen and his sons began an experiment with a Socialist community in New Harmony, Indiana in 1825. Advertisements announced the experiment for the cooperative colony, which required volunteers to work an 8-hour work-day of which Owen was a proponent. The town banned money and other commodities for barter, using "labor tickets" denominated in the number of hours worked.

Owen's son, Robert Dale Owen, would say of their failed Socialist experiment that the people at New Harmony were too eclectic to succeed; some were radical, some lazy, and others were devious. The larger community lasted only until 1827, at which time smaller communities were formed, as an attempt to keep the concept going. New Harmony dissolved in 1829 due to constant quarrels as parcels of land and property were sold and returned to private use.

The Anarchism of Mikhail Bakunin

Russian born Mikhail Bakunin (1814-1876), is considered the Father of Modern Anarchism. He was a libertarian Socialist, advocating for workers to directly manage industrial production through their own productive associations. The association would provide equal means of subsistence, support, education, and opportunity for every child, boy or girl, until maturity, and equal resources and facilities in adulthood to allow individuals to become self-sufficient.

While many Socialists emphasized the gradual transformation of society, Bakunin became disillusioned with the viability of that approach. He supported direct political action as the best way to build a collectivist state.

Bakunin traveled across Europe trying to stir up a Socialist revolutionary spirit while advocating the overthrow of the Russian Czar. Bakunin participated in the Czech revolution of 1848 and was arrested and imprisoned in Germany before being handed over to the Russian authorities. Returned to Russia, Bakunin was imprisoned by the Czar and exiled to Siberia. He escaped in 1861 and made his way to London via San Francisco and Boston. Bakunin attended the First Communist International in 1869 and was active in the Communist Party until 1872, when he was expelled by Marxists.

The Maturing of Economic Socialism

Karl Marx (1818-1883), and Friedrich Engels (1820-1895), developed a body of ideas they called Scientific Socialism, more widely known as Marxism, from Socialist concepts introduced during the French Revolution, as well as from the German philosophy of Hegel, the English political economy, and the writings of Adam Smith. Marxism comprised a theory of history as well as a political, economic and philosophical theory. In the *Manifesto of the Communist Party*, written in 1848, just days before the outbreak of the revolutions of that year, Marx and Engels wrote, "The distinguishing feature of Communism is not the abolition of property generally, but the abolition of bourgeois property." [8] Unlike those Marx described as Utopian Socialists, Marx determined that "the history of all hitherto existing society is the history of class struggles." While Utopian Socialists believed it was possible to work within or reform Capitalist society, Marx confronted the economic and political power of the Capitalist class, expressed in their ownership of the means of producing wealth. Marx and Engels formulated theories regarding the practical way of achieving a Socialist system; as only achieved if those who produced the wealth in society, the workers, could gain common ownership of their workplaces, the site of the means of producing wealth.

Marx believed that Capitalism could only be overthrown by means of a revolution carried out by the working class. He held that the proletariat was the only class with the cohesion,

---

[8] Karl Marx and Friedrich Engels. *The Communist Manifesto.* (Marx/Engels Selected Works, Vol. One, Progress Publishers, Moscow, 1969), pp. 98-137.

the means, and the determination to carry the revolution forward. Unlike the Utopian Socialists, who often idealized agrarian life and deplored the growth of modern industry, Marx saw the growth of Capitalism and an urban proletariat as a necessary step towards Socialism.

For Marxists, Socialism was the first phase of Communist society; it was a transitional stage characterized by common, or state, ownership of the means of production under democratic workers' control and management. This stage formed the connector between the Capitalist and Communist states. Because the Socialist phase had characteristics of both its Capitalist ancestor and the future Communist state, it would manage the means of production collectively, but it would distribute commodities according to individual contribution. When the Socialist state withered away, there would remain a society in which human beings no longer suffered from alienation and all the springs of co-operative wealth would flow abundantly. Here society functioned as: "From each according to his ability, to each according to his needs!"[9] For Marx, a Communist society entailed the absence of differing social classes and the end of class warfare. Once a Socialist society was created, the state

---

[9] Ibid.

would disappear and humanity would be in control of its own destiny for the first time in human history.

European Socialism after 1850

The word Socialism was not exclusive to the Left but was also used by Right wing Collectivists. They vigorously debated each other over who had the right to commandeer the term. Both those on the Right and the Left were anti-individualist; both advocated government management of the most important aspects of society; both divided human society into groups which they took to be fundamental to individuals' identities; both pitted those groups against each other to create conflict; both favored war and violent revolution to bring about the ideal society, and both hated Liberals. This period marked a return to Tribalist thinking in Europe. The Socialists were a large enough tribe to oppose the Enlightenment tribe with vigor. The Collectivists had developed many tools useful to attack Individualism. All that remained was to implement a system to replace it.

Right and Left Collectivists in Opposition

The events of the early 20th Century would ultimately settle the conflict between Left and Right-wing Socialists. In World War I, the philosophical battle would be waged between the Liberalism of the West and the Socialism of Germany. German intellectuals were confident that they could defeat decadent Liberalism and open the door for Right-wing Socialism to take over the world. Johann Plenge (1874-1963), an expert on both Hegel and Marx, asserted that Liberalism was corrupt and would be replaced by Socialism. Plenge also believed that Socialism would come to Germany first because Germany had long embraced Socialist dreams and possessed the temperament to make it succeed.

Germany's defeat in World War I was a significant blow to the collectivist Right. That defeat, and its psychological impact on Germany, led to the popularity of Oswald Spengler's book *The Decline of the West* (1914). In this book, Spengler described the failure of Germany to find its destiny. He believed that all Western institutions, from democratic government to Capitalism to the developments of technology, were decadent. He also believed that Mechanical Capitalism had won the battle to be the dominant economic system, even though it took over and stifled the freedom of the individual. This outcome could not be reversed.

Spengler published his next book, *Prussianism and Socialism* (1920), with a goal of trying to show that Socialism must come from within a national culture, not internationally, as Marx had suggested. Consistent with the Right-wing Socialist orthodoxy, Spengler argued that the state must be in control of production and society must bend to the operation of the state.

Speaking against Marxists, Spengler argued that their ideology shared responsibility with Capitalism for generating an overly materialistic world. He wrote later in *Man and Technics* (1931), that the Modern world was artificial and corrupting to the natural world. Civilization had become mechanical and dependent on machinery. Everything in sight became a technology, spoiling the natural beauty that exists in the world.

Although Spengler was pessimistic about Germany's future, other Right thinkers still believed in the Socialist ideal. Ernst Jünger (1895-1988), for example, became in inspiration to the Right. He understood that World War I had been lost, but this setback could be overcome. Jünger strongly believed that Germany should derive its energy to move forward from the defeat they had just experienced. Werner Sombart (1863-

1941), was another intellectual who believed in the Right-wing Socialist ideal. A Marxist for most of his career, Sombart moved toward the Right after he learned to accept the superiority of authoritarian Socialism. He argued that Socialism must be disconnected from Marxism in order to give it a national focus. Free of Marxism, Socialism could utilize nationalist sentiment to create a new set of ideals. Utilizing this energy and focus, Socialism would be prepared to battle its true enemy, Liberal Capitalism. Sombart's major work, *Merchants and Heroes* (1915), attacked Liberal Capitalism, presenting the German people as noble in comparison to the decadent states of the West. Profit was the enemy of a society and all economic systems based on profit, should be replaced.

Socialism had to prevail against this evil, but it must be Right-wing socialism, not Marxian Socialism. Right thinkers argued that Marxist Internationalism was not legitimate Socialism because it described a universalism that didn't exist. Right-wing Socialism would be the foundation of Germany's Third Empire. **This was a Tribal battle between German Left and Right-wing Socialists.** Eventually, one would devour the other.

Right-wing Socialism wins and then dies

During the 1920s, the stage was set for the upcoming ideological battle involving the burgeoning National Socialists, the Communists, and the German Social Democratic Party. The Social Democrats and the Communists disagreed whether Socialism would be achieved by evolution or revolution. The Social Democrats argued that there was no difference between the Communists and the National Socialists. Both favored violence rather than gradual change. The Communists argued that the Social Democrats and the National Socialists were both Capitalist models in disguise.

The differences between National Socialism and Communism boiled down to a choice between the dictatorship of the common people and the dictatorship of the workers. The blurring of differences between the parties resulted in alternating election victories with no clear winner emerging during the 1920s. Eventually, the National Socialists were able to build a power base among university students who saw themselves as rebelling against the ineffective Weimar Republic, forced upon them by the Liberal West.

As we know, Western Liberal civilization survived both the Great Depression and World War II, emerging stronger than it had been before. During the war and its aftermath, the National Socialists and the collectivist Right were wiped out physically and discredited morally and intellectually. The new battle lines were simplified and abundantly clear: it would be Liberal Capitalism versus Left wing Socialism.

POINTS TO REMEMBER

- Collectivism is an ideology that promotes groups as a more important component of society than individuals.

- The concept of Collectivism began with Rousseau who vigorously opposed the Enlightenment.

- After Rousseau, Collectivism took two different paths: Germany turned Right, and the rest of Europe turned Left.

- Kant began the path of the German Right with his assertion that the individual was insignificant in the world.

- Kant was followed by Herder, who argued for a unified German nation and Fichte who agitated for a common educational model for Germans to understand their place in history.

- Left-leaning Collectivism began in France with Saint-Simon and evolved through utopianism and anarchism to reach the economic Socialism of Marx.

- Left versus Right Socialism reached a climax in World War II when the Right-wing Socialism of the Nazis was wiped out and discredited.

CHAPTER SEVEN

THE FALL OF SOCIALISM

Socialism is a philosophy of failure, the creed of ignorance, and the gospel of envy, its inherent virtue is the equal sharing of misery. **Winston Churchill**

The collapse of Socialism as a viable political system occurred gradually as its implementation couldn't outperform the success of the Capitalist model. Socialism proved to be an impractical economic system, so its promise of greater equality never materialized. Socialism's failure, however, should not be confused with a loss of popularity. There continues to be a strong following for the Socialist ideology. Its adherents believe there will come a time when Socialism will be accepted and implemented by some future enlightened society. Even, today in the United States, it remains popular. Bernie Sanders lists his party affiliation as Socialist and he is poised to make a second attempt to win the Democratic nomination for president as such. Of course, Bernie is always careful to make sure his brand of Socialism is not the same as the historical model, which has been fully discredited.

Starting in the middle of the 19th Century, and on into the 20th, the hopes and dreams of Socialism's believers were thwarted by its lack of success. During the second half of the 20th Century, when reality revealed that Socialism was a failure, the efforts of those who remained loyal were redirected toward criticizing and changing Capitalism. For two centuries, the Left's intolerance of inequality has hindered them from accepting Capitalism as the political system most compatible with human behavior.

Socialism in Germany

Germany had the strongest Socialist movement in Europe during the 19th Century. After 1864, when Germany was first united, the development of trade unions generated strong pressure on the evolving German state. Carried along by the growing nationalist tide, the Socialists organized a political party, positioned themselves to gain power and sought to transform Germany into a Socialist political system. Their opponents were Liberals, who were pushing for the formation of a parliamentary government, conservatives supporting the status quo, and Catholics, who wanted to have a say in the government of the Reich. Although the Socialists had the largest growth in representation between 1870 and 1912, their early designs on power were foiled by Otto Von Bismarck (1815-1898). Arguably the greatest German statesman of all time, Bismarck dominated the affairs of Germany and Western Europe for thirty years, between 1860 and 1890. In his role as Minister President of Prussia, Bismarck united the German nation in 1871, and for the next twenty years engaged in diplomatic efforts to keep a balance of power between Germany and the rest of Europe.

Bismarck realized that if he could embrace key parts of the Socialist's agenda, he could disrupt the party's momentum, so he broke his alliance with the Liberal party and aligned himself with the center Catholic Party. That alliance allowed him to implement the beginning of a welfare state, offsetting the key plank in the Socialist Party platform. Bismarck built the German welfare state operating from the Right, which relieved the pressure applied by the Socialists. While he was doing so, the conservative landowner class made sure that the social changes did not interfere with their traditional conservative power base.

Germany was in a unique position that facilitated its move to a welfare state. After the Thirty Years War, Prussia began building its own army, which was unusual at the time. Most of the German states employed mercenaries. The Prussian army had its own bureaucracy separate from the government. When the Prussian leaders converted to Calvinism, they became motivated to build a new social bureaucracy that would create and manage new institutions such as schools and housing for the poor. In the beginning, the social bureaucracy was patrimonial but, over time it transitioned to a system where participation was based on merit. Later, when the Prussian government moved in the direction of democracy, the new political parties protected the social bureaucracy from having its power marginalized. While the parties fought for power, and were held back by Bismarck, the bureaucracy continued on. Eventually, the welfare state initiatives came under the control of the bureaucracy which rendered them permanent and stable.

Socialist Failures

From the German point of view, World War I was a test of Socialist ideology against Enlightenment Liberalism, which Germany had never accepted. The Germans assumed that Liberalism would not be able to stand up to an authoritarian political system. Defeat at the hands of the Allies was a shock that forced the German Left to question those beliefs. By the 1920s, Marxist Socialism faced a set of theoretical problems. Why had the predictions of revolution not come to pass? The exploitation and alienation of the people were obvious and clearly had an impact on the victims of Capitalism. Still, there was no revolution.

In Russia, Lenin had to amend Marxian theory to account for the differences between Russia and the classic Marxian model. Russia, as a feudal society, had never reached the Capitalist state that Marx required in his model of Communist transition. Lenin knew he didn't have time to develop a Capitalist model so he had to make the revolution work without one. That could only be accomplished by creating a new class of Socialist elites who could impose the Communist doctrine on the Russian people through whatever means necessary. As the world now knows, Russia evolved into an authoritarian dictatorship which was Marxist in name only.

A New Approach

In Germany, the German Social Democrats (SPD) were ineffective. They were the leading Socialist party in the world and in control of the German government in the first two decades of the 20th Century, but were unable to expand Socialism to a statewide political system. Party intellectuals decided that Socialism needed a new direction and new leadership that would set a new course for the Socialist ideology. That new course would need an intellectual foundation. which had been lacking previously.

The answer to that need came in the form of the Frankfurt School, an educational institution of social theory and philosophy associated with the Institute for Social Research at the Goethe University in Frankfurt. The Frankfurt School has had an enormous influence on Socialist thinking from its founding in 1923 until the present.

The school was made up of neo-Marxist dissidents who were intellectually uncomfortable with the Capitalist, Fascist, and Communist systems operating at the time. Many of these critics believed that traditional theory could not adequately explain the turbulent and unexpected development of Capitalist societies in the 20th Century, given their inherently dehumanizing and exploitive characteristics. Critical of both Capitalism and Soviet Socialism, their writings sought an alternative path to socio-political development.

The Frankfurt School

Responding to the alienation and irrationality in an advanced Capitalist society, the Frankfurt School developed Critical Theory as a comprehensive, ideology-critical, historically self-reflective philosophical tool with a dual purpose. First, it sought to explain domination in human society, why class separation and alienation exist. Second, it wanted to explore the possibility of bringing about a rational, humane, and free society. Frankfurt School theorists developed numerous hypotheses and principles of the economic, political, cultural, and psychological structures to explain the advanced industrial civilization.

A principal focus of the Frankfurt School was the creation of a new discipline called Critical Theory, which Max Horkheimer (1895-1973), one of the school's leaders, introduced in his 1937 book *Traditional and Critical Theory*.

Critical Theory had two objectives: to unmask the lies generated by bourgeois society which justified the domination of people by Capitalism and to explain areas of Socialist ideology that Marx had not dealt with.

Horkheimer argued that the scientific methodology applied to the physical sciences could not be used in the social sciences because the researchers themselves were "social." In other words, they lost objectivity when their personal ideas influenced their work. Social science researchers lived in the historical context of their own discipline and this shaped their thinking. Horkheimer's solution to this dilemma was Critical Theory, which is the reflective assessment and critique of society and culture using knowledge from the social sciences and the humanities. To overcome the problem of subjectivity in social scientific inquiry, Critical Theory placed itself "outside the box".

Horkheimer maintained that Critical Theory should concentrate its focus on the totality of society in its historical context. To improve understanding of society, Critical Theory had to integrate all the major social sciences, including geography, economics, sociology, history, political science, anthropology, and psychology. While

Critical Theory must always be self-critical, Horkheimer insisted that a theory is critical only if it is explanatory. Critical Theory must, therefore, include practical thinking to explain what is wrong with current social reality, identify actors to change it, and provide clear norms for criticism and practical goals for the future. In Horkheimer's words, the goal of Critical Theory was to release mankind from the circumstances that have kept him captive.

Frankfurt School theorists tied themselves to the critical philosophy of Immanuel Kant, who used the term "critique" to mean philosophical reflection on the limits of claims made for certain kinds of knowledge, and on the direct connection between this type of critique and the emphasis on man's moral decision making. Using this intellectual context, Critical Theorists sought to rehabilitate Marx's ideas through a philosophically critical approach.

Critical Theory rejected the materialism of orthodox Marxism. The material tensions and class struggle of which Marx spoke were seen as no longer having the same revolutionary potential within contemporary Western societies. This observation asserted that Marx's interpretations and predictions were either incomplete or incorrect. Frankfurt School theorists would correct Marx by arguing that when action fails, the theory guiding it must be reviewed. In other words, Socialist philosophical thought must have the ability to criticize itself and repair its own errors. While theory must drive practice, practice must also have a chance to drive theory.

Hope for Victory

The Great Depression in the United States brought hope to the Socialists and motivated them to seize the opportunity to move their agenda forward. Their wish was that the Depression would provide the motivation for a revolution of the downtrodden working class in the United States. This did not happen. Equally alarming was the rise of National Socialism in Germany and Italy where movement leaders were able to convince their public that an authoritarian approach to government founded and built upon a Right-wing Socialist ideology was superior to that of Socialism on the Left.

It was the Left-wing Socialist's hope that their enemies on the Right and the Liberals would kill each other off during World War II and leave the Left-wing Socialists to take over. Of course, that was not what happened. Right-wing

Socialism was destroyed, and the Liberal West emerged from the war stronger and more self-confident than ever before. This mixed blessing left the Socialists with a single competitor, but it was a formidable one.

During the 1950s, the Left was still under the illusion that the Soviet Union would prove itself economically against the West, demonstrating the value of the Marxian model, but Soviet "five-year plans" failed to produce the results they were looking for. Once the Left understood that the Soviet Union could not win economically, it decided to focus on equality as the desired outcome. The hope was that the Soviet Union might still succeed as a morally legitimate ideology.

That myth died when Soviet Premier Nikita Khrushchev gave a secret speech to the Soviet Party Congress on February 25, 1956 in Moscow, outlining the crimes of Stalin. In October of that same year, the Soviets brutally suppressed an uprising in Hungary. It was now plain for all to see that the Soviet Union was nothing more than a violent authoritarian dictatorship in Socialist clothing.

Disappointment over the Soviet failure caused many Leftists to embrace Mao, the leader of China, in the hope that his model would succeed where the Soviet Union had failed. Again, there was only disappointment when the death toll of 36 million people from Mao's forced famine of 1959-61 became public. Belief in the Maoist ideology was permanently damaged.

These crises of the 1950s forced most Left intellectuals to recognize that the case for Socialism was in serious trouble economically and morally. They realized that making the case for Socialism was doubly difficult because the Capitalist countries were doing well economically and, for the most part, going in the right direction morally. It was hard to argue with prosperity, and it was hard to make criticisms about Capitalism's moral status stick, compared to the revelations about the horrible and very real failings of Socialism in practice.

A new ethical standard for Socialists

At the party conference of the German Social Democrats (SPD) in November 1959, a new program was introduced. The Godesberg Program was designed to recast the Socialist ideology from a defender of the poor and impoverished, as described in Marxist theory, to a party representing all the people.

The Godesberg Program was notable because it abandoned and rejected Marxist theories of materialism and class struggle. This meant also that the SPD dropped its hostility to Capitalism, which had long been the core of its ideology. Socialism now moved beyond its working-class base to embrace all voters. This new strategy featured a political ideology grounded in ethical appeals. Labor unions abandoned the old demands for nationalization and instead cooperated increasingly with industry. Union leaders achieved labor representation on corporate boards and garnered increases in wages and benefits. The SPD, after losing national elections in 1953 and 1957, moved toward an American-style, image-driven electoral strategy that stressed personalities. One of the most notable individuals during this period was Berlin Mayor Willy Brandt. As it prepared for elections in 1961, the SPD dropped its former opposition to rearmament and accepted NATO. Prior to that point, the SPD had always adhered to the Communist Party edict that it opposed all institutions that represented the West.

Another approach, originating in the Frankfurt School, featured a new definition of "poverty", which the Left began to circulate in the early 1960s. It abandoned the claim that Capitalism would generate a revolutionary proletariat based on the exploitation of the working class. Instead, the people would become revolutionary because they would see that others in society had greater wealth than they did. This wealth inequality would prove psychologically oppressive as opposed to economically oppressive, resulting in a revolution.

While traditional Communist theory was universal across societies and within them, Left thinkers and activists began to break universalist concepts down to a focus on special interest groups, specifically women and racial minorities. Again, the focus continued to highlight equality, not class identity. This appeared to be a winning strategy, because it was hard to argue that women and racial and ethnic minority groups had made significant gains in Capitalist nations. These groups were not being driven into poverty, but they were not being lifted out of poverty either. Women and minority groups were clearly denied the same opportunities available to white men.

Attack on Wealth

The Left's attack on wealth involved a more audacious change of ethical standards than had been tried previously. Traditionally, Marxist Socialism had taught that providing adequately for human needs was fundamental to a social system's morality. Based on that assumption, wealth was good. As it became clear that Capitalism was very good at producing wealth, and that Socialism was failing to deliver, the Left decided to turn the argument around. Capitalism was corrupt because it produced wealth. The new ideal was to live simply and avoid producing or consuming too much.

Marcuse and the captive class

In the 1960s, the increasingly popular writings of Herbert Marcuse (1889-1976), added to the evolving ideology of the Left. Marcuse was the member of the Frankfurt School who gained the greatest prominence in the English-speaking world, especially North America. Politically, he was a Marxist dedicated to embedding the Marxist belief system into the Capitalist model.

Members of the Frankfurt School had looked for ways to replace the "class struggle" ideology of Marx. They expanded their thinking beyond Marx's social model and sought an answer in psychology. Freud was the prominent psychiatrist of the time so Horkheimer and others used Freud's concepts to develop a new approach. Marxism had overlooked the fact that those who would begin the revolution possessed psychological drives that influenced their behavior. Without the right psychological thinking within and among its leaders, the revolution could never be realized. The Frankfurt School theorists began to use Freud's *Civilization and its Discontents* as a resource for their thinking. Freud saw human society as the suppressor of man's animal nature which demanded immediate gratification and behaved without discipline. While society helped to control man's base instincts, it also suppressed those traits and related behaviors that were important to exercise. Freud suggested that the best way to understand these suppressed urges was to draw them out using non-rational mechanisms, including dream analysis and hypnosis.

The Frankfurt School theorists believed that modern Capitalist society suppressed the natural state of humans by creating an artificial world of machines and bureaucracies. These systems removed man from nature and forced him into an artificial existence. This new existence destroyed the spontaneity and creativity of human beings. More importantly, people were unaware this was happening to them.

Marcuse asserted that the wealth Capitalism produced was the oppressor of the proletariat. By making the members of the proletariat wealthy enough to become comfortable, Capitalism had made them into a captive economic class. Once part of the system, the proletariat found themselves locked into a "dog eat dog" existence, constantly competing with their neighbors. Trapped in this process, they were distracted by material and trappings of a Capitalist society, accepting the Capitalistic notion that possessions had value. That distraction posed a threat to the achievement of a Socialist reality. If only the chains of oppression could be removed from the backs of the workers, they would be free to pursue a life of Socialism. It was the task of Socialist intellectuals to explain how the working class was being exploited so they could see the truth and use it as motivation to achieve a Socialist reality.

The Environment as an Issue for the Left

Another post-Marxian strategy involved the Left connecting

to the environmental movement in the 1960s. As Leftist intellectuals searched for new ways to attack Capitalism, the environment was added to the list of focus points, which already included women and minorities.

Traditional environmental philosophy was consistent with Capitalism. As Teddy Roosevelt promoted it, America was a place of beauty and that beauty should be preserved. The influence of man on the environment was positive; man changed his natural environment to make the world more productive. Sometimes compromises had to be made, resulting in a short-term negative impact on the environment, but in the long term, a healthy economy was compatible with a healthy environment. Moreover, an increase in wealth would generate the dollars needed to protect the environment.

Marxists came to realize how they could use the concepts of exploitation and alienation by applying them to environmental issues. Mankind, which had developed the capability to rule the earth, caused great harm to the planet and all living things on it. In the same way that Capitalists exploited minority groups, they exploited the resources of the earth and did irreparable harm to it. The link between human behavior and the health of the planet was forever perilous and fragile and would never be broken. Capitalism meant the production of wealth, and wealth necessitated exploitation of the environment, so Capitalism was the enemy of the environment.

Changing Socialism's focus

Along with the redefinition of Marxian theory and the new Socialist ideological connection to Freud, the Left began to move away from the Rationalism of Marx. Following Freud, they came to believe that in an unpredictable world, practical ideologies had to incorporate non-scientific social theories, such as Freud's hypnosis, into their thinking. This direction was developed in the 1930s, but ignored for the next two decades. There were just too many matters to address, including the development of National Socialism in Germany, World War II, and the Cold War, which was driven by classical Marxist theory.

By the 1950s, there were two factors that began to change Socialist thinking about non-rational ideas. First, academics in American and Western Europe became skeptical about the power of reason. The dead end of Logical Positivism showed that logic was useless in explaining human knowledge. The popularity of Heidegger and his Phenomenological ideas demonstrated this move against Rationalism. Secondly, classical Marxism had failed and, it too was based on Rationalism. These conclusions led to the emergence of non-rational Socialism.

The wholistic Marxist movement split into sub-movements emphasizing the Socialism of sex, race, and ethnic identity. No longer was there a view that workers across the globe were the appropriate target group. That concept was discredited as an idealistic classical conception. The Socialists needed a rational approach to uniting the Modern world, so Rationalism had to be pushed aside.

Without reason, there was no mechanism to convince the masses to unite across the globe and change the world. The task was just too difficult. What the masses could understand were their sexual, racial, ethnic, and religious identities. The limits of Socialist theory and the desire to match communications to the audience dictated a move from universalism to multiculturalism. This emerging New Left principle was consistent with the ideology of the Collectivist Right. The Right had long argued that human beings were not fundamentally rational. For political progress to be made, it was essential to appeal to and utilize the irrational passions of the people. Many in the new generation of Socialists absorbed this new ideology and sharpened their swords.

Terrorism

In the late 50s and early 60s, five elements combined to ignite a more violent, terroristic, Leftist effort. These elements were: 1) the academic climate against reason; 2) impatience about the revolution; 3) extreme disappointment at the failure of the Socialist ideal; 4) hatred of the success of Capitalism, and 5) justification of irrational violence based on the writings of the Frankfurt School.

The founding dates of some of these terrorist groups are obscure. All were explicitly Marxist Socialist, and none had existed prior to 1960. Some of the groups also had strong nationalistic overtones.

In addition to the five factors listed above, several important events served as triggers for the upsurge in violence. Among the far Left, the death of Che Guevera in 1967 and the failure of the 1968 student demonstrations in most Western nations, especially of the student revolts in France, contributed to radical's anger and disappointment. Several of the terrorist manifestos published after 1968 make explicit mention of those events, as well as reflecting the broader themes of irrational will, exploitation, decent from beauty to commodity, rage, and the need to do something. For example, Pierre Victor (1945-2003), the leader of the French Maoists with whom Michel Foucault was associated, hearkened back to the French Revolution's Reign of Terror and declared that instituting a brief period of terror was entirely justified if it was directed against a handful of contemptible, hateful individuals.

Other terrorists cast their nets more broadly. Before her death, Ulrike Meinhof (1934-1976), made very clear the broad purpose of the Red Army Faction she and Andreas Baader (1943-1977), founded in Germany: "The anti-imperialist struggle, if it is to be more than mere chatter, means annihilation, destruction, the shattering of the imperialist power system—political, economic and military"[10].

---

[10] Ulrike Meinhof in Stephen Aust. *Baader-Meinhof.* Translated by Anthea Bell, 1987. (Oxford, Oxford University Press, 1985). p. 202.

Meinhof also made clear the broader historical context which made terrorism necessary.

> Nauseated by the proliferation of the conditions they found in the system, the total commercialization and absolute mendacity in all areas of the superstructure, deeply disappointed by the actions of the student movement and the Extra-parliamentary Opposition, they thought it essential to spread the idea of armed struggle. Not because they were so blind as to believe they could keep that initiative going until the revolution triumphed in Germany, not because they imagined they could not be shot or arrested, not because they so misjudged the situation as to think the masses would simply rise at such a signal. It was a matter of salvaging, historically, the whole state of understanding attained by the movement of 1967/1968; it was a case of not letting the struggle fall apart again. The rise of Left terrorism in nations other than those controlled by explicitly Marxist governments was a striking feature of the 1960s and early 1970s. Combined with the broader turn of the Left to non-

Rationalism, irrationalism, and physical activism, the terrorist movement made that era the most confrontational and bloody in the history of the Left Socialist movements of those nations.[11]

But the Liberal Capitalists would not be soft and complacent. By the mid-1970s, police and military forces had defeated the terrorists, killing some, imprisoning many, driving others underground, more or less permanently. The prominent terrorist organizations were dispersed by the mid-1970s and terror lost its momentum when the Viet Nam War issue was settled.

From the collapse of the New Left to Postmodernism

With the collapse of the New Left, the Socialist movement was dispirited and in disarray. No longer were they waiting for Socialism to materialize. No one thought it could be achieved by appealing to the electorate. No one was able to mount a coup. And those willing to use violence were dead, in jail, or underground.

---

[11] Stephen Aust. *Baader-Meinhof.* Translated by Anthea Bell, 1987. (Oxford, Oxford University Press, 1985). P. 204.

What then was to be the next step for Socialism? In 1974, Herbert Marcuse was asked whether he thought the New Left was history. He replied: "I don't think it's dead, and it will resurrect."

During the 1970s, as the New Left collapsed, it turned to those best able to think strategically, those best able to situate the Left historically and politically, and those most up to speed on the latest trends in the philosophy of knowledge. Foucault, Lyotard, Derrida, and others started executing a new Left vision. Accordingly, it was those philosophers who led the invasion into American Academia. Their strategy was to use words instead of weapons. Words must be used against Capitalism regardless of their meaning or truthfulness. Once Academia was turned, the next target would be politics. **Postmodernism would become a tool of** the Socialists, who became determined to destroy Capitalism when their dream of a Socialist world did not come to fruition.

During this time of retrenchment for the Socialists, Tribalism was fermenting in the United States. The Marxist emphasis on Identity Politics and the environment began to attract those who wanted to advance these agenda. The Left needed an ideology to embrace and moved toward an Anti-universalist vision of small group representation, abandoning the universally oppressed class.

POINTS TO REMEMBER

- At the turn of the 20th Century, Germany had the strongest Socialist system, built to rival Liberalism for control of the political ideology of the West.

- The defeat of Germany in World War I showed Socialism's inferiority to Liberalism and led German intellectuals to rethink Marx.

- A new program, Critical Theory, was created by the Frankfurt School in Germany in the 1920s and was an attempt to bring Marx's theory up to date.

- In 1959, the German Socialist movement adopted the Godesberg Program, which refocused Socialist efforts toward defeating Capitalism. Rather than class politics, it opened itself toward the goal of equality for everyone. Socialist programs were now tied to ethical issues.

- The Left also began to focus on groups of human beings (identities), such as women and African-Americans.

- A prominent spokesman for the new Socialist approach was Herbert Marcuse, a member of the Frankfurt School. Marcuse claimed that the price of the accumulation of wealth in the West was a captive lifestyle that enslaved people to the quest of economic success. Now wealth had become a bad word.

- The collapse in confidence in the Socialist revolution spawned spontaneous attempts at revolt in the 1970s. The Bader-Meinhof group in Europe and the Weathermen in the United States were examples of groups who attempted to create revolutionary conflict. By the end of the decade, they had been suppressed.

- In the 1980s, when Socialism became discredited and the revolts were put down, the Left turned to Postmodernism as a substitute for the Socialist ideology.

- In America, Postmodernism invaded academia.

CHAPTER EIGHT

THE DEATH OF REASON

He that cannot reason is a fool. **Andrew Carnegie**

The 20th Century saw the most radical changes in man's philosophical inquiry into truth and knowledge since the Enlightenment. Arguments about the value of reason as a tool for establishing truth came under attack and then reached a dead end. This collapse of reason opened the door for Postmodernism to establish itself in American academia. Postmodernism contributed to the Tribalism that haunts our country today.

Until the Enlightenment, philosophy was considered the gateway to knowledge. All forms of inquiry began with the philosophical disciplines of Natural Philosophy and Natural History. Natural Philosophy focused on a theoretical study of the world. The study of physics was an obvious example. Natural History was focused on describing objects in the world, such as plants and animals, which could be characterized by collecting data about them. Later, Natural Philosophy would become physics and chemistry, while Natural History would become the biological sciences and geology. The foundation of Natural Philosophy was reason, which allowed man to acquire knowledge about his relationship with the outside world. Reason was the power of comprehending, inferring, or thinking in rational ways, in order to obtain truth. European scholars, prior to the Enlightenment, accepted reason as the only path to the truth. As we mentioned before, they believed reason could be used to access the truth without the existence of data to support their conclusions.

As the Enlightenment unfolded, scholars began to subject all knowledge to a new level of scrutiny. They attacked historical belief systems and forced them to prove themselves. Any idea that could not survive the attacks, would be discarded.

The Enlightenment and its establishment of the scientific method had a profound impact on philosophy. Because Science that provided the basis for the development of technological systems, its function moved it beyond the capability of Natural Philosophy. What remained for the philosophers to think about were the questions that science either couldn't address or had no interest in addressing; What is knowledge? What is being? Does God exist?

A philosophical struggle began in earnest over reason, sense data from the real world, and truth. That struggle has lasted until the present day. One might think about these issues and say, "Who cares about the accuracy of our perceptions of the world? We use our daily experiences to guide us through life. Isn't contemporary philosophy only an exercise for scholarly debate?" The answer is "No" because the results of that scholarly debate spread into the public sphere. The answer is "No" because the impact is far subtler than the more practical disciplines and occurs over a longer span of time. Its final audience is the public institutions, where philosophical ideas influence public policy and lead it in new social or moral directions.

20th Century American Philosophy

For most of the 19th Century, American philosophy took a different path than philosophy in Europe. The Anglo-American tradition had always championed the Enlightenment Project and was enamored with science, reason, and objectivity. Academicians rejected ideologies that were not consistent with this view. They sought to turn philosophy into a scientific endeavor and justify its foundation.

Positivism

Positivism was a philosophical theory asserting that knowledge was based on natural phenomena and all their properties and relationships. Information derived from sensory experience was interpreted through reason and logic, and formed the exclusive source of all knowledge. Positivism held that true knowledge was found only in this verified knowledge. Data received through the senses were known as empirical evidence, so Positivism was based on Empiricism.

Positivism also held that society, like the physical world,

operated according to general laws. Introspective and intuitive knowledge were rejected, as were any principles unverifiable by sensory experience. Positivism had been a recurrent theme in the history of Western thought long before it was adopted in America. The modern version was formulated by Auguste Comte in the early 19th Century. Comte argued that just as the physical world operated according to gravity and other absolute laws, so did society. In his view, Positivism applied to the social sciences as well as to the physical sciences. That meant that logic could explain human behavior in addition to the physical world.

Positivism fit well into American thinking because it came out of the Enlightenment view of science. America was born during the Enlightenment and stood as one of its greatest achievements, so there was a natural commonality between American ideas and science. Unlike Europe, the United States did not have to replace medieval thinking to embrace science, so the new American perspective made it possible for Positivism not only to be accepted, but also to prosper.

In the 20th Century, Positivism gained a new direction based on innovations in logic and mathematics. This new focus began when Bertrand Russell brought evolving

German ideas to the English-speaking world. He published a book with A. N. Whitehead titled *Principia Mathematica* (1910-1913). Russell's work on logic and the philosophy of logic was one of the approaches that led to the creation of the successor to Positivism, called Logical Positivism.

Logical Positivism

According to Logical Positivists, a statement was meaningful only if it was either purely formal (essentially, mathematics and logic) or it was capable of empirical verification. This point of view resulted in a nearly complete rejection of the study of "being" on the grounds that it was unverifiable. Logical Positivism was also committed to the idea of "unified science", or the development of a common language with which all scientific propositions could be expressed.

Russell summarized the history of philosophy as a repeating series of failures to answer its questions. Was it possible to prove there was an external world? No. Was it possible to prove there was cause and effect? No. Was it possible to validate the objectivity of inductive generalizations? No. Was it possible to find an objective basis for morality? No.

He concluded that philosophy could not answer its questions, so it must be removed from attempts to determine truth or wisdom. Ludwig Wittgenstein (1889-1951), and the early Logical Positivists agreed with Russell, taking his conclusions one step further in describing philosophy's failure: philosophy could not answer its questions because they were simply meaningless. Moreover, philosophy's questions were beyond unanswerable, they were not even intelligible.

Earlier philosophers had mistakenly thought philosophy was about its own unique subject matter. It was not. Content such as metaphysics, ethics, theology, and aesthetics were all meaningless exercises. To make philosophy useful, its function had to be redefined. Philosophy was not a content discipline, it was a method discipline. The function of philosophy was analysis and nothing more.

Another name for Logical Positivism was "analytic" philosophy, pointing to its purpose of analyzing the perceptual, linguistic, and logical tools that science used. Scientists perceived and organized their observations linguistically, using specific concepts and propositions, and then structured those linguistic units using logic.

Philosophy's job was to figure out what perception, language, and logic were all about.

These conclusions about logic were a threat to science; if logic was divorced from reality, it could not be used to describe reality. The implication was that logical proofs could not help us decide the truth when we looked at competing claims of fact. Since analytic propositions were devoid of factual content, no experience could prove they were wrong. Accepting that propositions of logic were not based in experiential reality led us to question where logic came from. If there was no objective source, then the source must be subjective. That meant it could not be used to help us understand the world. That conclusion, after decades of work, was that our perceptual intuitions did not conform to objects; our intuition conformed to what our knowledge supplied from itself. Consequently, all the work done in Logical Positivism was useless because it had nothing to do with reality.

In Chapter Three we discussed the Counter Enlightenment and its philosophical contributors. The early concept of reason as intuitive was challenged by Hume and others who showed that our perceptions of the world were unreliable.

Kant separated unreliable perceptions from "things unto themselves" holding that man could not disprove the existence of God. Hegel got beyond Kant's skepticism by creating a system that allowed man to arrive at truth through a process of analysis. That did not satisfy the irrational philosophers, Kierkegaard and Nietzsche, who believed that feelings and faith were the only ways to reach the truth. The next link in that chain was Martin Heidegger.

Heidegger anticipates Postmodernism

Martin Heidegger (1889-1976), like his immediate predecessors, believed that reason was an unreliable method of arriving at the truth. Rather than moving in the direction of the Positivists, he extended the ideas of Kierkegaard and Nietzsche, the irrationalists who proceeded him. Heidegger asserted that man could get closer to the essential being than Kant allowed, using a method that would become known as phenomenology. Heidegger agreed with Kierkegaard and Schopenhauer that by exploring one's feelings, especially the dark and anguished feelings of dread, one could understand the true self.

Heidegger saw the fundamental problem of Western Philosophy as the answer to the question "What is being?"

What does it mean that humans are beings? What separates us from the objects in nature? The term "human being" describes us but is not the essence of us. What then is inside us? Heidegger invented the word Da-sein (sein is German for "to be") which for him was the pathway to understanding the real essence of human life. Dasein was the portal through which we communicate to the outside world.

Heidegger's method of communicating to the real world was called phenomenology, a theoretical view that took ordinary experience as its point of departure. Through an attentive and sensitive examination of each experience, phenomenology aimed to reveal the original core of the conditions that shaped it and gave it structure. To use the phenomenological method, a person manipulated the environment around them, to experience a "logic free" pathway to the inner meaning of being.

Here is a simple example of how this worked. A carpenter wanted to cut a board in half with a saw. The board and the saw served as his equipment. He started cutting and, while doing so, he entered a phenomenological state. The motion of his arms, his sense of being a person, and the world around him all disappear. All that remained was the phenomenological union of man and equipment. The carpenter remained in this state until the board was completely cut. Then he returned to the reality of his being.

Heidegger's principles were esoteric, they were the stuff of philosophers trying to make logical sense of the world. Still, his efforts were just another example of the thoughts man had struggled with since he developed the capability to contemplate his own existence. Heidegger approached phenomenology because of the ideas that came before him.

Heidegger concluded that reason was subject to a specific set of principles. Conflict and contradiction were the **deepest truths of reality, so when man sought truth, it became easy to get confused. Reason was subjective because** the way we approached truth depended on the circumstances that existed at the time. Words and concepts were only symbols representing objects and bore no resemblance to the objects they represented. Deep emotions, such as despair were more real than attempts to reason. Heidegger believed that all Western Philosophy, prior to his time, had failed because it never was able to understand the real core of being.

The End of Reason

By the 1950s, most philosophers considered language and logic to be conventional, internal systems, not objective, reality-based tools of consciousness. Heidegger's drift off into an emotional dark sense of being was just another dead end.

A decade later, with the publication of his landmark book, *The Structure of Scientific Revolutions* in 1962, Thomas Kuhn announced that progress of Analytic Philosophy had ended. Kuhn asserted that the tools of science were an evolving, subjective project, with changing views of objectivity. The idea that science represented true reality was an illusion.

The stage was now set for the growth of Postmodernism and its invasion of American academia. Postmodernism grew out of a philosophical wasteland in which the principles of truth and how to obtain it could not be determined. Philosophers had tied themselves in knots over this critical principle and ended up at a dead end. Now it was impossible to establish the circumstances under which knowledge of the real world could exist.

The Postmodernists discarded Heidegger's ideas of knowledge and his mysticism. Their anti-realist beliefs told them that Heidegger was wasting his time trying to find truth through understanding being. They rejected the idea that conflict and contradiction were the **deepest truths of reality.** Instead, they asserted they were nothing more than descriptions of what life was like in the real world. They understood that words and concepts were obstacles to knowledge, but they did not believe these obstacles could be overcome in a search for ultimate understanding.

The Postmodernists built their system on the backs of Heidegger and Nietzsche. Both philosophers believed that one could not obtain knowledge without rejecting reason. The Postmodernists discarded Heidegger's phenomenology and replaced it with Nietzsche's "will to power". At the same time, they discarded Nietzsche's celebration of human potential and replaced it with Heidegger's view that humanism was a corrupt ideal.

POINTS TO REMEMBER

- Philosophy, as it related to man's understanding of being and knowledge reached a dead end in the mid-20th Century.

- Kant had begun the decline by showing that knowledge was questionable because our perceptions of the world were unreliable.

- What later followed were the irrationalist philosophies of Kierkegaard and Nietzsche, who rejected the concept of reason. Faith, feeling, or instinct were the only ways to discover reality.

- American philosophy took a different path and relied on a scientific approach to philosophical problems. Positivism, Logical Positivism, and Analytic Philosophy each expressed the American connection to science.

- The 20th Century saw the phenomenology of Heidegger take center stage. His belief was only through the phenomenon of exploring one's own feelings, could a person discover reality.

- By the middle of the 20th Century, all forms of Positivism had reached a dead end, because they were no longer able to show any connection between logic and reality. That meant the Anglo-American world was now susceptible to the siren song of the Postmodernists.

CHAPTER NINE

POSTMODERNISM

Postmodernism entices us with the siren call of liberation and creativity, but it may be an invitation to intellectual and moral suicide. **Gertrude Himmelfarb**

In the previous chapters, we have detailed the history of the Enlightenment; how it began, the factors that influenced it, and its impact on the modern Western world. Immediately and ever since, there was a reaction against its accomplishments. It was attacked initially for destroying religion and attempting to sweep away the traditions of Western Europe. These attacks were unsuccessful because they failed to blunt the human drive toward freedom for the individual, the advancement of science, and the implementation of Capitalism.

We have also detailed the history of Collectivist thought, which has traditionally stood in opposition to freedom for the individual. Collectivist ideas bore two children; the Right-wing authoritarian model of the Nazis and the Left-wing economic model proposed by Karl Marx. Both failed. The authoritarian model was buried with the collapse of the Nazi regime; its shameful genocide etched forever in human history. The economic version lasted longer but was unable to show that it could compete with Capitalism. It failed as an economic system in the disastrous Five-Year Plans of the Soviet Union. It failed as an ideology when Mao starved millions and the Soviet Union attacked Hungary in 1956.

Chapter Eight, The Death of Reason, described the debate over truth and reality that began during the Enlightenment and reached a dead end in the 1950s. Philosophers, seeking ways to find the ultimate truth and the genuine reality came up empty. The collapse of reason was one of the sparks that fueled the Postmodern phenomenon.

At the endpoint of the debate about reality stood Martin Heidegger. Writing in the mid-20ᵗʰ Century, Heidegger told us the only way to truth was through phenomenology, which was the analysis of the structure of human consciousness and the objects of human awareness. To him, truth lay only inside the phenomena.

The path to Postmodernism was laid wide open. It was a fast-paced modern world with a growing human feeling of isolation, minority groups demanding freedom and equal rights, and a frustrated Progressive Movement, forced to abandon its attachment to the Socialist model and left with no ideology upon which to build its future. The timing was perfect for a new set of ideas to take hold. Those ideas came from France and the men who defined and espoused them seemed to accurately describe the world of the 1970s in a way that would resonate in the United States.

French Philosophy in the mid-20ᵗʰ Century

In the mid-20ᵗʰ Century, avant garde philosophy returned to France. The 150-year gap from Descartes and Rousseau to the French philosophers of the 20ᵗʰ Century, had been dominated, in Europe, by German philosophy. Now, two new philosophical systems appeared: Existentialism and

Structuralism. Although Kierkegaard originated it, Existentialism was most often associated with Jean-Paul Sartre, the French author, playwright, and activist. Existentialism was described by the phrase "existence proceeds essence", meaning humans were independently acting beings who could think, reason, and understand the world on their own. Labels, roles, or stereotypes, which were used to define human beings, were not reality. Human beings, through their own consciousness, created their own values and determined the meaning of life.

Structuralism: Reducing knowledge to logic

Structuralism was derived from Kant's philosophy and held that language was a self-contained non-referential system. The philosopher's task was to seek out the necessary and universal features, which formed the character of language. Proponents of structuralism argued any subject could be understood by means of a language structure, which combined reality and imagination. In Jacques Lacan's (1901-1981), *Psychoanalytic Theory*, the structural order of "the Symbolic" was distinguished both from "the Real" and "the Imaginary." Similarly, in Louis Althusser's (1918-1990), *Marxist Theory*, the structural order of the Capitalist mode of production was distinct from both the actual, real agents involved in its relations, and from the ideological forms in which those relations were understood.

Poststructuralism to Postmodernism

By the mid-20th Century, Structuralism came under severe criticism by the French philosophers Jacques Derrida (1930-2004), and Michel Foucault (1926-1984). They rejected the foundation of Structuralism and were later labeled Poststructuralists. They believed knowledge could not exist separate from the individual, because experience created knowledge and everyone's experience in the world was different. Knowledge cannot be based on either external structures or personal experience, but must be a combination of the two. These "Poststructuralists" suggested that by analyzing and deconstructing linguistic structures, one could come to understand how history and culture have influenced those structures.

Poststructuralism

Poststructuralism was an ideology that followed Structuralism and questioned accepted ideas about truth, reality, meaning, and good. It regarded all absolutes as constructions. Truth was created, rather than present or inherent *in* something. Furthermore, there was no such thing as authority. Everything was defined in relation to everything else, and that process itself was relative and constructed.

The key philosopher for the poststructuralists was Nietzsche, who asserted "God is dead, and we have killed him" so anything was possible, everything was permitted, everything was relative. Nietzsche made this statement as an indictment of the Enlightenment's destruction of religious tradition. Religion had provided the structure for man's morality over the course of the history of mankind; without it, man stood at the brink of disaster. To the Postmodernists, this realization set the stage for a new view of the world, a view that stood in opposition to the Enlightenment.

As the Poststructuralist movement was growing in popularity in the 1970s, other socio-historical events were taking place, some on their own merit but all acting together. The radical political groups from the 60s (for example the Maoists) were coming to an ideological dead-end. Alexander Solzhenitsyn's (1918-2008), works were in translation and revealed in detail the horrors of the Soviet Union. The importance of the media as agents for social change was being realized and media saturation was becoming an important cultural phenomenon.

As a result, there was a backlash against Marxism and Socialism. It was argued that Marxism was a system whose intellectual totalitarianism must lead to the Gulag. Now, Liberalism and Capitalism were embraced as being more open and relevant. Intellectuals moved away from political engagement and back to "intellectual" work. Those thinkers took a great interest in the role of the media in defining reality for contemporary society. They looked at society as fragmentary, full of images, and saturated by media that made everything relative, ephemeral and short-lived… in other words, postmodern.

Postmodernism

It is difficult to define Postmodernism. It grew out of Poststructuralism but was something different, even though the two systems were closely connected. First and most important, Postmodernism was an attack on the Enlightenment and the modern world it created. The foundational components of the modern world, including Individualism, Capitalism, Liberalism, and the industrial society, were targets.

The goal of Modernism was to show that science and reason could solve the problems of mankind by explaining the world. That made sense; the ways human beings were linked together in society was obvious to all, and the goal of improving the lives of people was worth the effort.

Modernism suggested that humans could understand and fix a chaotic world that had existed beyond human control. Even though the marketplace was cruel and unforgiving, man could use reason and knowledge to understand its workings. He could then develop the systems needed to manage society to benefit all people. This required a belief in science and its ability to accurately describe the real world.

The Enlightenment's twin ideologies, Socialism and Liberalism, emerged as solutions to the problem of controlling Capitalism. Each believed it was focused on the correct unit of society, Socialists on the class or group, and Liberals on the individual. Both were committed to a grand narrative that included exclusive adoption of their ideology to benefit human society.

Postmodernism rejected the Enlightenment Project and all that came out of it. Postmodernists believed that foundational ideas, such as political ideologies, were a tragic human mistake that could never have worked. Their evidence was based on 20th Century changes in human society. We lived in a period of discontinuity caused by changes in communication and the pace of life. Postmodernism accepted this new world and became part of it, rather than resisting it.

Postmodernism announced a rejection of abstract reasoning and deep resentment toward any project seeking to advance the human condition through the powers of science. Those on the Left understood, since Socialism and Modernity were connected, the rejection of the Modern Age forced the rejection of Socialism as well. In the purest sense, that left the world with Nihilism – the belief that nothing matters. Postmodernism as a cultural movement, believed that "anything goes".

The Postmodernists

Jean-Francois Lyotard (1924-1998), was a philosopher, sociologist, and literary theorist. He was educated initially at the Sorbonne and eventually received a PhD in philosophy. He taught in French Algeria and later supported that country's effort to gain independence. Lyotard had

Socialist/Marxist sympathies, including participation in the French Revolt of 1968, but later moved away from Marxism. He held a faculty position at the University of Paris from 1972 to 1987, and later, lectured around the world.

Lyotard labeled Modernity as the age of legitimizing meta-narratives and regarded Postmodernity as the age in which metanarratives became obsolete. He described the Postmodern Age as one of fragmentation and division into groups. Lyotard identified the status of knowledge and its legitimization as the fundamental problem for society. Knowledge created power, so these terms were closely interrelated. In the Information Age, those who held the data held the power. Lyotard further argued that changes in knowledge during the Postmodern period allowed the knowledge holders to legitimize the knowledge they controlled when it suited their purposes. Consequently, there was no consensus as to the truth. He predicted that someday control of information would lead to war.

Lyotard believed that science was legitimated by one of two metanarratives. The first predicted the totality and unity of all knowledge, with scientific advancement leading society to that goal. The second suggested that science would lead to the emancipation of humanity. Since the Postmodern world assumes that metanarratives were now dead, science could only be legitimized by its performance in an operating economy.

Michel Foucault

Paul-Michel Foucault, generally known as Michel Foucault, was a French philosopher, historian of ideas, social theorist, and literary critic. He completed his PhD in 1960, after spending nine years teaching in Sweden, Poland, and West Germany. Foucault was a member of the Communist Party from 1950-53, later rejecting Marxism. He held faculty positions and published many books before his death in 1984. Foucault wrote a history of the French penal system and a history of medicine, using history to show how social conditions were perceived differently over time. For example, the insane were locked up in the Middle Ages, but in the Modern Age, a set of pathologies was invented and used to remove the mentally ill from society. Groups were excluded from the Enlightenment when they didn't fit its definition of inclusion.

Foucault may be best known for his writings on power. In his book, *The Will to Knowledge*, which focuses on power and power relations, Foucault stated that knowledge was incomprehensible apart from power and, in his writings, replaced the Marxian belief in class power with the idea of power knowledge. The problem, Foucault pointed out, was the public's negative conception of power, which labels it as something that must be prohibited. That way of thinking ignores the influence of power on behavior. Foucault claimed that all previous political theory viewed power as connected to an absolute monarchy. We imagine power as something individuals could possess, and could organize pyramidally, with one person at the top. That was power operating by handing out punishments, but power was more often relational and people exercised it, based on their interactions with others. Power had its own behavior, which emerged from the actions of people within a network of power relationships.

This logic led Foucault to analyze the specific historical dynamics of power. Biopolitics invested people's lives at a biological level, which made us live according to norms, in order to regulate humanity at the level of the population. Behind that stood the politics of administering death, exaggerated into industrial warfare that killed millions. This power was taken from the people and used against them.

Jacques Derrida

Jacques Derrida was one of the most well-known 20th Century philosophers, publishing more than 40 books, together with hundreds of essays and public presentations. He had a significant influence upon the humanities and social sciences, including philosophy and literature. Derrida wrote and published on many philosophical topics but he is most well-known for his innovative approach to analyzing texts.

With his detailed readings of works from Plato to Rousseau to Heidegger, Derrida argued that Western philosophy uncritically allowed textual complexity to govern its understanding of language and consciousness. This "logocentrism," he argued, created binary oppositions that have an effect on everything from our conception of speech's relation to writing to our understanding of racial difference. Examples of these binary oppositions are man/woman, large/small etc. These dualisms privilege the first word and make the second word subordinate to it. That relationship is the result of Enlightenment constructed hierarchy. The subordinated word, as in the pair, man/woman, carries a context that woman is inferior to man.

Derrida invented Deconstruction as a tool to expose and undermine false dualism. It operates through a sustained analysis of specific texts and uses the analysis to look for places within the text that point towards alternative meanings. It then identifies alternative and repressed meanings so they can be brought to the surface and connected to the text in a new way. Invention was an important part of the deconstruction and the analyst was free to speculate on alternative meanings. The False dualisms, Derrida identified, privileged specific groups in society to the exclusion of others and granted them power they didn't deserve.

Deconstruction became a boon for English and Literature departments in universities because it created a theory of language that they could use in the same way that science utilized the scientific method.

Why did Postmodernism Emerge?

Postmodernism found a place in 20th Century America because it appeared to understand and explain American culture better than alternative belief systems. The age of hyper-communication had significantly impacted political and economic practices, the balance between the classes, and cultural and social life. The speed of communications disrupted mankind's ability to function through thoughtful planning and careful implementation of new ideas.

The Postmodernists asserted that the disruption did not fit the Enlightenment model of a slow steady progress of mankind. The Enlightenment model was now obsolete and needed to be replaced by another model that could be used to lead humanity forward.

Postmodernism's influence has gone beyond the impact technology has had on the speed of our lives. It has impacted the historical consensus about what constitutes knowledge, the value of science, and our ability to reason. Uncertainty in these areas has raised anxiety about the future and has pushed us into a tribal mindset, reverting to a social structure that is more comfortable.

Interactions between people in this Postmodern Age involve increasing numbers of impersonal anonymous communications, none of which possesses a personal aspect, like shared values, traditions, or points of view. In these impersonal anonymous communications, there is a pervasive loneliness, that is not able to satisfy the human need for fulfilling social interactions. Each one of us has become an island in an impersonal world.

POINTS TO REMEMBER

- In the 1970s, Postmodernism began from the ideas of a group of French Poststructuralists, who had abandoned Marxism. Lyotard, Foucault, and Derrida were its champions.

- Postmodernism strongly rejected the ideas of the Enlightenment. It was marked by the renunciation of foundational thought, of the rules governing art, and of the ideologies of Liberalism and Marxism. Lyotard defined Postmodern as "*incredulity toward metanarratives*," and suggested the incredulity was such that we could no longer expect Liberalism and Marxism to successfully lead mankind into the future.

- In philosophy, Postmodernism announced a rejection of abstract reasoning and deep antipathy toward any project seeking universal human emancipation through mobilization of the powers of technology, science, and reason. Those on the Left understood, since Socialism and Modernity were connected, the

176

rejection of the modern also rejected Socialism. In the purest sense, that left us with Nihilism – the belief that nothing matters. Postmodernism as a cultural movement, believed that "anything goes".

- The emergence of Postmodern thinking has been attributed to a crisis in which space and time, as we experience them, are compressed in a way that human beings cannot tolerate. This compression has had a disorienting and disruptive impact upon political-economic practices, the balance of class power, as well as cultural and social life.

- The hi-tech revolution, mass media, consumerism, and modern communications have contributed to the emergence of Postmodernism.

CHAPTER TEN

THE ROAD TO POSTMODERNISM IN AMERICA

The Enlightenment is under threat. So is reason. So is truth. So is science, especially in the schools of America - **Richard Dawkins**

The history of philosophy in America was unlike that of the European Continent. Born during the Enlightenment, the American Colonies absorbed modern thinking, and the founders applied Locke's philosophy to the design of our federal government. America's founding, during the Enlightenment, implemented its major ideas as a great experiment in individual freedom.

The 19th Century American Philosophy

During the 19th Century, new philosophical approaches appeared in America. The first was Transcendentalism, which developed out of the Romantic movement. It was based on the idea of subjective, personal experience being superior to experimentation. The belief was that a transcendental state extended human experience beyond the physical and empirical. To reach this state, one had to locate a place where moral reflection was possible without interruption. That place was in nature where one could interact with the plants and animals that share the environment. The most famous proponent of this philosophy was Henry David Thoreau (1817-1862), whose two-year occupation of a small cabin at Walden Pond, near Concord Massachusetts became a part of American folklore. Thoreau and the writer Ralph Waldo Emerson (1803-1882) were the leaders of the Transcendental Movement.

After Darwin's work on evolution was published, some Americans suggested that our own philosophy be viewed through the lens of evolution. The American philosopher, William Graham Sumner (1840-1910), was its greatest proponent. Sumner, along with the industrialist Andrew Carnegie, believed that laissez-faire Capitalism was the most natural approach to a political-economic system, because it accurately emulated life in the wild.

The most important philosophical trend in the United States in the 19th Century was Pragmatism. Its most well-known adherents were Charles Sanders Pierce (1839-1913), William James (1842-1910), and John Dewey (1859-1952). Pierce, who was a major contributor to the scientific method, coined the term Pragmatism in 1870. He believed the concept of an object consisted of the sum total of its observable effects. For example, if a ball bounces, then it has the property of bouncing. That property and any others man identified made up the practical nature of the object.

William James was a philosopher and psychologist, commonly called "the Father of American Psychology." He characterized Pragmatism as promoting not only a method of clarifying ideas but also an endorsement of specific theory of truth. James was also known for his radical empiricism, holding that relations between objects were as real as the objects themselves. James was a pluralist and believed that multiple accounts of truth could exist. He also believed that truth encompassed a belief, facts about the world, and future consequences of that belief.

John Dewey, the third founder of Pragmatism, had a significant presence in the public sphere as a Progressive activist. Dewey argued against the individualism of classical Liberalism, asserting that social institutions were not means for obtaining something for individuals, they were means for creating individuals. Dewey was well known for his work in the applied philosophy of education. His beliefs promoted the idea that children learned best by doing. Dewey also believed that schooling was unnecessarily long and formal, and that children would be better suited to learn by engaging in real-life activities.

Analytic Philosophy

As we discussed in Chapter Six, Analytic Philosophy was another major current in American philosophy from the 19th Century through the middle of the 20th Century. It was made up of home-grown Positivism followed by an imported version of European Logical Positivism. The latter was an attempt to use logical and mathematical principles to prove the truth of philosophical questions. Logical Positivism proved to be a dead end when its proofs were unable to provide a connection to the real world. That dead end created a problem for the concept of reason.

Political Philosophy in the United States

Political philosophy in the United States was dormant from the time after the new government was put into place in 1787 until the mid-20th Century. It then resurfaced with the work of Ayn Rand, who promoted ethical egoism (she called it Objectivism) in her novels, *The Fountainhead* (1943), and *Atlas Shrugged* (1957). These books gave birth to the Objectivist movement that influenced a small group of students called "The Collective". One member of the Collective was Alan Greenspan, a self-described Libertarian who would later become Chairman of the Federal Reserve.

Objectivism held that there was an objective external reality that could be known with reason. It required human beings to act in accordance with their own rational self-interest above the interest of groups. Rand believed the proper form of economic organization was laissez-faire Capitalism, which was the most efficient economic model. Later philosophers were highly critical of the quality and intellectual rigor of Rand's work, but she remains a popular figure within the American Libertarian movement.

In 1971, the academic philosopher John Rawls published *A Theory of Justice*, in which he laid out his view of creating an ethical government using the concept of "justice as fairness," built on a combination of liberty and equality. Rawls employed the use of a conceptual mechanism called the "veil of ignorance," to demonstrate his idea. To properly build a government, a group of creators would be employed to design its structure. They would set aside all biases resulting from their own traits or opinions about the world because they would not know which characteristics they would receive. For example, the new government could not be biased against women because the designers would not know if they would be female or male. Rawls felt that the veil of ignorance would ensure the creators took into account those who would be worst off in society to protect themselves.

The resulting government would be based on two principles. First, each person was to have an equal right to the most comprehensive bias-free system of equal basic liberties that were compatible with a system of universal liberty. Second, social and economic inequalities were to be arranged so they provided the greatest benefit to the least advantaged human beings. Rawls put liberty above equality to make sure that attempts to level the economic status of a society did not harm liberty. With liberty intact, economic equality would be achieved through the redistribution of wealth.

Rawls' system was based on Analytic Philosophy and appealed strongly to the Left because of its equality of opportunity overtones; Rawls became enormously popular in the United States and Europe during his lifetime.

Viewing Rawls as promoting excessive government control and rights violations, Libertarian Robert Nozick published *Anarchy, State, and Utopia* in 1974, which advocated for a minimal state and defended the liberty of the individual. Nozick argued that the role of government should be limited to basic services like police protection and national defense. The rest of what we commonly consider part of government, like education, would be taken over by private institutions.

Alasdair McIntyre (1929-), born and educated in the United Kingdom, spent forty years living and working in the United States. McIntyre, writing mainly in the 1980s and 1990s was responsible for the resurgence of interest in virtue ethics, a moral theory first promoted by the ancient Greek philosopher Aristotle. McIntyre's view was that modern philosophy and modern life were characterized by the absence of any coherent moral code; the majority of individuals living in this world lacked both a meaningful sense of purpose in their lives, and a sense of community. McIntyre recommended a return to genuine political communities where individuals could be exposed to and build their own morality. His positions appealed to those who rejected the ability of analytical philosophy to understand morality.

By the 1970s, the United States floundered in a state of confusion with several political ideologies in opposition. Analytical philosophy remained strong, but there was no consensus on ideologies that would govern truth, knowledge or being. The door was open for something new that could appeal to the Left by filling the void created by the collapse of Socialism. That set of ideas would have to accurately describe the discontinuity of the time and stake out a new position. Postmodernism would be the ideology to fill that void.

Postmodernism's arrival in the United States
The French Postmodernists, who came to the United States in the 1980s and shared their views on American college campuses, seemed to understand the turmoil in the United

States. American academics, activists, and authors were drawn to Postmodernism because it explained shifts in social issues and sought to analyze elements the American society that had not been looked at before. These included living, lifestyles, and relationships. It was in that context that Postmodernism took its place in American society, from campuses to social movements and across the intellectual space.

Barbara Epstein, Professor Emeritus at UC Santa Cruz, has described the emergence of Postmodernism as follows.

> Many feminists and gay and lesbian activists became interested in the work of Michel Foucault, because his focus on the social construction of sexuality, view of power, and insistence on the connection between power and knowledge, made an impression on them. These groups saw Foucault's work as providing a theoretical ground for moving away from a focus on the economy and the state (Socialist theory), to the social relations between people and the problems of daily life. Foucault viewed state power as repressive and his kinship with the

marginalized and suppressed rang true at a time when radical struggles were being led by groups outside the mainstream of culture and power relations, such as disaffected youth and women, blacks and other racial minorities, gays and lesbians.[12]

She also describes how Postmodernism connected itself to the cultural and political currents in place at the time. This was most notable in architecture and art where it described the way the new world could be represented. At the same time, popular culture was applying so much pressure on the concept of art that it only made sense to merge it with traditional art. The explosion of media and its subsequent relentless impact on the American society helped validate the Postmodernist view of a world of confusion, fragmentation, and barriers to validating truth. These features became attached to those of popular culture including distraction, disconnectedness from the past, and a sense of meaninglessness. Postmodernists successfully described the world in a way that other ideologues could not.

---

[12] Barbara Epstein. 1997. *Postmodernism and the Left.* (New Politics, V. 6 No. 2, No. 22, Winter, 1997). p. 6.

Both Socialism and Liberalism depended on an accurate understanding of society in time so that solutions for improvement could be validated against reality, but in the 1970s that understanding seemed to have disappeared.

Many American academics did not embrace Postmodernist thinking. To those individuals and groups, Postmodernism seemed too trendy and in love with the chaos it had created, as if the pleasure of destruction was more important than solving the problems of society. Moreover, Postmodernism seemed to shift cultural values regardless whether the new values fit any specific set of problems. Its celebration of the fragmentation of self and society ignored the need for balance. Those on the Left who resisted the pull of Postmodernism remained focused on identity politics or retained their traditional Socialist ties.

As time moved on, and especially in the early 1990s, Postmodernism became associated with avant garde or trendy currents. It acted out its new role by adopting criticism for its own sake. It became a thing unto itself and moved away from its connection to social movements. New links were created with academia so Postmodernism expanded its position in elite universities. There, it became subject to the increasingly harsh and competitive world of research and the need to "publish or perish." That required Postmodernism to stand out, to bring attention to itself, and a new radical behavior became its approach of choice.

Much has been written about the two "types" of Postmodernism: strong and weak. Each has found a following for different reasons. The strong version, as you may imagine, takes the more extreme positions of the French Postmodernists. For example, the belief that truth does not exist was at the center of its view. Because all perception was mediated by individual differences or communication between different personalities, claims of truth were only claims, not reality. There was no way to measure these truth claims because they were subjective, and nothing stood outside of the them to determine their validity. That meant that all claims of truth must have equal standing. The strong position took the form of an extreme social constructionism. It asserted that political positions were constructed entirely through interpretation; there was no identifiable social reality against which interpretations could be judged.

Reasonable people might agree that perception was mediated by one's environment but disagree that the results of perception led to the equal status of all claims to the truth. They would also agree that even if ultimate truth was elusive, it was still possible to expand our understanding of the world and expand our knowledge, to the benefit of mankind. As science would put it, any state of knowledge was subject to revision when contradictory facts become available. For obvious reasons, this strong version of Postmodernism was not popular and lived mainly in academic debates rather than in the real world.

The "weak" version of Postmodernism had a more solid connection to reality and argued that language and culture played a role in shaping societal attitudes. One had to be careful not to assume that socially constructed ideas were naturally occurring. This approach was both logical and valid. The difference between the two versions was the zeal of the strong version and the trap it created for itself. Since it tried to make culture the focus for the explanation of human behavior, it took the position it criticized in the Enlightenment, namely that it was a grand narrative.

The postmodernist critique of the Enlightenment is one-sided. It discards the beliefs that a universal view of humanity was a reaction against narrow nationalism, when it uses truth to tear down oppression by resisting official claims that government is right.

Problems with the Postmodernist subculture have been defined succinctly by Barbara Epstein, when she described the trendiness of Postmodernism. That trendiness begets an intellectual arrogance along with an obscure vocabulary. There is a faddishness that adores the new and is self-congratulatory. Postmodernism identified research as identified as revolutionary and unique, conducted only in the hope of achieving fame. On the other side is bullying and ridicule of any counter belief, similar to the behavior of the Left when it was defending Socialism for most of the 20th Century. As with Socialism, the tribe of Postmodernists was held so tightly, that any association with the non-believers would give one a "traitor" status.

Similar behaviors emerged in the women's movement, including definitions of Feminism that saw men as an enemy who should be opposed at every turn. This feminist dogma did not allow for any competing points of view.

In the cases cited above, the Left in the United States has tended toward idealism that is not grounded in the practical.

Terry Eagleton (1943-), has argued that Left intellectuals in the United States have adopted Postmodernism following Socialism's defeat by Capitalism; this generated the belief that the Left, as a political force, had little future. Culturalism, Eagleton argues, involved an extreme subjectivism, a view of the intellect as all-powerful, and that, combined with a deep pessimism, gave a sense that it was meaningless to learn about the world, because it can't be changed anyway.

Progressive Divide

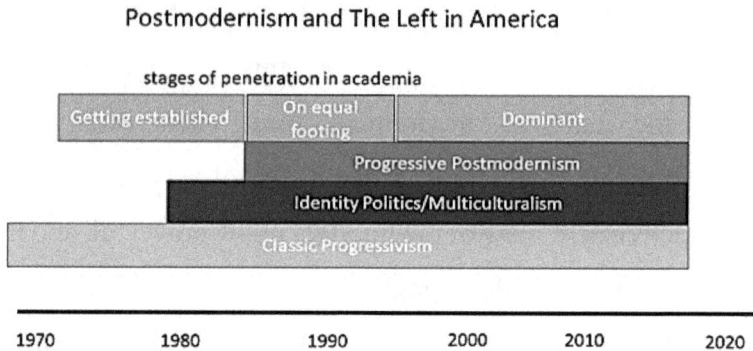

Postmodernism and The Left in America

stages of penetration in academia

Getting established	On equal footing	Dominant

Progressive Postmodernism

Identity Politics/Multiculturalism

Classic Progressivism

| 1970 | 1980 | 1990 | 2000 | 2010 | 2020 |

Over the last 50 years, the Progressive Movement has split into three parts. Postmodernism syphoned off a portion of Progressives who were attracted to its description of a confusing Postmodern world. Part of the remainder stayed connected to identity politics/multiculturalism concerns, perhaps substituting for the loss of Socialist ideology. The rest remained classic Progressives, including the old time Socialists.

194

POINTS TO REMEMBER

- Political philosophy was dormant in the United States from the time of the American Revolution until the 1970s.

- It was awakened in the 1960s by political and social concerns about our changing society.

- Ayn Rand and John Rawls are examples of new political thinking in the period between the 1950s and 1970s.

- American political philosophy was overwhelmed when Postmodernism was introduced into American academia in the 1970s by the French Postmodernists.

- Many feminists and gay and lesbian activists became interested in the work of Michel Foucault, because his focus on the social construction of sexuality, view of power, and insistence on the connection between power and knowledge, intersected with their own concerns.

- These groups saw Foucault's work as providing a theoretical ground for shifting the focus of radical analysis away from the economy and the state (the historical components of Socialist theory), to the social relations between people and the typical problems of daily life.

- The excitement of postmodernism was based on its links to vital cultural and political movements, and the fact that it was pointing to rapid changes in culture and examining these through the poststructuralist categories of language, text, and discourse.

- Many American academics did not embrace Postmodernist thinking. To those individuals and groups, it seemed too trendy and in love with the chaos it had created.

- By the late 80s and early 90s, Postmodernism was taken over by the pursuit of the new or avant-garde. Radicalism became identified with criticism for the sake of criticism and equated with intellectual or cultural sophistication. Postmodernism became a thing unto itself, moving away from its ties to actual social movements.

- Two versions of Postmodernism have been described: a strong version that denies the existence of truth and a weak version that asserts that claims of truth must be scrutinized.

- It has been argued that the Left intellectuals in the United States have adopted postmodernism out of a sense of having been badly defeated by Capitalism, a belief that the Left as a political force has little future.

- Postmodernism is a criticism-centric ideology, that avoids any commitment to a path for the future.

CHAPTER ELEVEN

THE DAMAGE

The biggest problem facing our world today is a lack of hope and a lack of meaning. [It's] basically just a postmodern world in which there is no right or wrong, no better or worse.
Jon Foreman

Tribalism has done a great deal of damage to American society, to American politics, and to the public's sense of well-being. The media reminds us hour-by-hour how divided we are, and are complicit in overemphasizing the divide because it profits them. The internet is also a significant factor, because everyone gets a voice and extremists have a forum. There is no filter, so the truth is difficult to identify. It's easy to exist in the day-to-day because new truths appear with the click of a mouse, but the drumbeat of negativity becomes more and more unsettling.

Tribalism has made Americans afraid to express their opinions, because they don't know how those opinions will be received. "What if I attack the Right at a party and someone on the Right overhears me and starts an argument?" "What if I, as a Progressive, express support for a Conservative idea and someone on the Left overhears me? They'll accuse me of being disloyal." Communication outside the tribal echo chamber is non-existent and people only listen to and speak to their own tribe.

Postmodernism became a major contributor to the Tribalism in America when it replaced the Left's Socialist ideology. In that guise, Postmodernism works to destroy all that is familiar and fosters the notion that "nothing matters." Postmodernism discards history and all the Enlightenment has accomplished, glorifying power as the most important human goal. Because grand narratives are dead, ideology is local and focused on groups, not individuals. Truth does not exist, and the idea that those in power positions have the right answers is a lie.

It's easy to feel Tribal when the glue that holds us together as a nation has been worn away. Until America is united again, the Tribes will rule.

Changing Political Parties

Starting in the 1970s, there were changes to the ideologies of the American political parties. Those changes arose from Right-wing attacks on the failures of the Liberalism of Lyndon Johnson, and led to the development of Neoliberalism and Neoconservatism. On the Left, there was backtracking from the failed welfare state, leaving an opening for the hibernating Progressive Movement to be awakened again.

Neoliberalism is a Right-wing ideology that believed wasteful government spending was ruining the American economy, so steps had to be taken to right the ship. Neoliberals emphasized the value of free market competition and moved the federal government toward that objective. They followed the views of Friedrich Hayek, the Austrian born Laissez-faire economist and author of *The Road to*

Serfdom. Hayek argued that government intervention, conducted with the idea of redistributing wealth, led to Totalitarianism. Neoliberals believe in Globalization, which it creates important economic benefits for the world powers.

In opposition to Neoliberalism, but still coming from the Right, was the Neoconservative ideology. The Neocons, which included many ex-Socialists, were disillusioned with the leftward move of the Democratic Party in 1972. Their key issue was foreign affairs and the need for the United States to be more interventionist than the country was in the 1960s and 1970s. Embedded in this ideology was a moral purpose to restore the vital ideas and faith that had made the West great in the past. The Neocons sought to prevent the emergence of any world power that would replace the fallen Soviet Union and it was this group that pushed George Bush into Iraq and other foreign entanglements.

While the new Right-wing ideologies were maturing, the Democratic Party passed through a crisis period, trying to redefine itself. Out of power from 1980 to 1992, the Democrats were able to elect Bill Clinton as a "new way" candidate. Clinton was able to navigate to a successful presidency from the middle of the political spectrum and avoid ideological commitments, but he did not repair the crisis.

Some argue that the collapse of the Soviet Union in 1989 deconstructed the Left-Right party polarity, emptying it of meaning. Ambiguous Tribalism replaced class politics, based on a reaction against Neoliberalism and a world defined by market economies. This phenomenon was fed by and also drove Postmodernism with its emphasis on cultural fragmentation and identity politics.

The Left saw Postmodernism as pointing out Neoliberalism's inability to preserve cultural differences while the Right used Postmodernism as a tool to critique Neoliberalism. The Right believed that cultural fragmentation and de-politization of the global society was detrimental to the aims of a unified state.

Starting in the middle of the Clinton presidency, the Republican and Democratic parties began a descent into a Tribalist opposition, as seen below. By 2014, center groups had disappeared and only the more extreme elements remained.

Democrats and Republicans More Ideologically Divided than in the Past

Distribution of Democrats and Republicans on a 10-item scale of political values

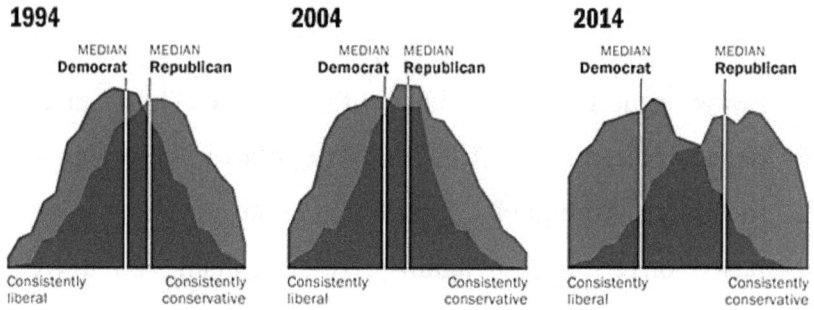

Source: 2014 Political Polarization in the American Public
Notes: Ideological consistency based on a scale of 10 political values questions (see Appendix A). The blue area in this chart represents the ideological distribution of Democrats; the red area of Republicans. The overlap of these two distributions is shaded purple. Republicans include Republican-leaning independents; Democrats include Democratic-leaning independents (see Appendix B).
PEW RESEARCH CENTER

One cannot place blame for this polarization on the parties; they do not lead ideological movements. The parties merely reflect the movements that are operating in American society by riding on the energy they create.

Positioning Ideologies

When observing this American Tribalist state, it's important to understand the difference between ideology and politics. Ideologies are a part of politics but have a different spectrum. Ideologies can contribute to Tribalism when they are divisive.

Political Party Spectrum

Progressive	Liberal		Conservative

Independent

Ideology Spectrum

Socialist (group egalitarian)	Liberal (individual)	Fascist (group authoritarian)

LEFT   RIGHT

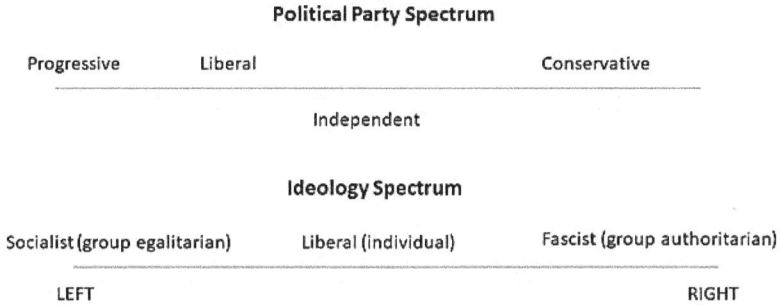

The political party spectrum has Progressives and Conservatives as opposites. This identification is based on the degree of desire for change. Conservatives want the status quo and Progressives want to change the status quo into something better. Progressives and Conservatives also have differing moral views of the role of government. Progressives are focused on social justice and equality; Conservatives are focused on national unity and efficient government. Progressives today are divided: some embrace Postmodernism, while others are repelled by Postmodernism but embrace identity politics or multiculturalism.

On the ideology spectrum, there are two Socialist groups: left Socialists (Communists) and right Socialists (Fascists). These Socialist alternatives appeared in the 19th Century as branches of collectivist thought. Liberalism, whether it is the classical version, or the modern "Neo" version sits in the middle. Liberalism is focused on individual rights, whereas the Socialist ideologies are focused on group rights.

Conservatives are not Fascists. Trump is not a Fascist. He's not even a Conservative. He's a Populist and Populists are politicians who don't embrace a particular ideology but build a platform around what they think the people want. In Trump's case, he appealed to groups that felt unrepresented and won the election by advocating for those groups.

Describing the Tribes

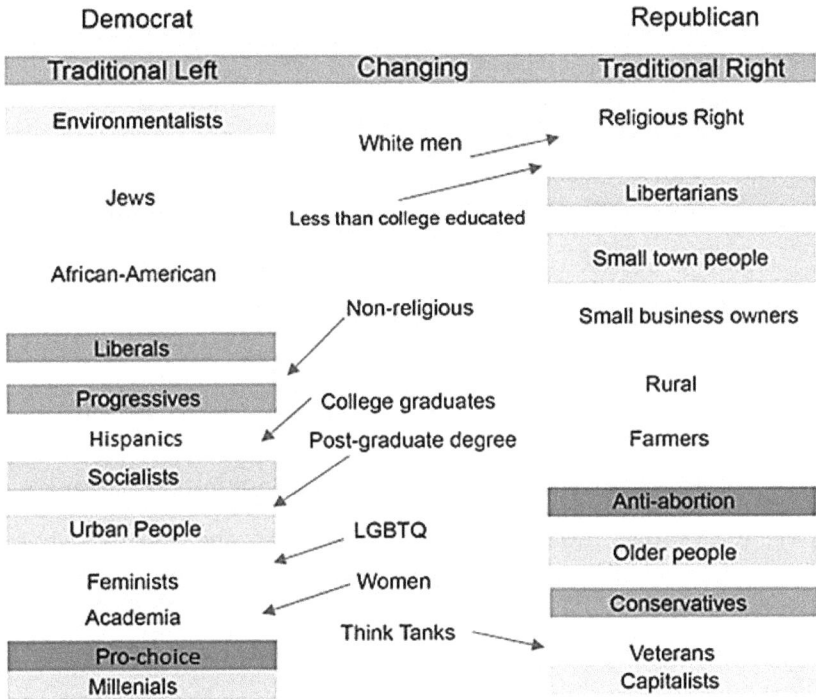

Democrat		Republican
Traditional Left	**Changing**	**Traditional Right**
Environmentalists		Religious Right
	White men →	
Jews		Libertarians
	Less than college educated	
		Small town people
African-American		
	Non-religious	Small business owners
Liberals		
Progressives	College graduates	Rural
Hispanics	Post-graduate degree	Farmers
Socialists		
		Anti-abortion
Urban People	LGBTQ	
		Older people
Feminists	Women	
Academia		Conservatives
	Think Tanks →	Veterans
Pro-choice		Capitalists
Millenials		

The left and right columns on the chart above show the groups supporting each political party.

Some groups have longstanding affiliations with one party or the other, but there are also groups who were located in the middle during previous decades but have moved to the Left or Right. Those migrations expand Tribalism as the center shrinks and communications between the sides evaporate. The value of the center is its impartiality. Since center groups contain both Left and Right leanings, they could act as a bridge between the tribes. Without an engaged center, the links between Left and Right disappear.

Distribution and Movement

If we think of the chart with Modern Liberals and Progressives on the left and Conservatives on the right, it represents the classic American ideology distribution.

Progressives have always embraced Socialist ideologies, so both of those groups live on the left. Modern environmentalism is a Socialist ideology designed to attack Capitalism, so it is foundational to the Left. Feminists and their pro-life programs, African-Americans, and Hispanics represent the principle identity groups of the Left. African-Americans supported Republicans in large numbers until the New Deal Era when they began moving to the Left. Then, starting in 1960, when the Civil Rights initiatives of the Johnson administration were resisted in the South, Southern whites became Republican and African-Americans embraced the Democratic Party in much greater numbers.

Academics have been moving to the Left for fifty years. Universities now have very few Conservative faculty members. (see Academia discussion below).

Jews have long had an affinity with Socialism. They supported Roosevelt for opposing the Nazis even though they typically promote socialist ideologies. Jews tended to distrust the conservative establishment as anti-Semitic.[13]

Millennials have a high preference for the Democratic Party because of their social justice, environmental, and equality concerns.

Urban dwellers have always leaned Left because of union membership and social and economic justice concerns.

On the traditional Right sit religious fundamentalists, rural populations, Libertarians, and pro-life groups. Capitalists have traditionally been located there but that may be changing with the "New Tech" revolution.

---

[13] Edward S. Shapiro. *Why are so many Jews Politically Liberal?* (MyJewishLearning.com, 2019)

Groups in the center have been on the move. Working class whites and the less-educated voted for Trump in 2016 because they saw him as representing their interests. They have felt marginalized in the Postmodern world because Progressives have abandoned them.

Party preferences for non-religious individuals have moved significantly toward the Democratic Party in the last twenty-five years. Today, three times as many non-religious Americans support the Democratic Party than support the Republican Party.

Likewise, educated people have been moving to the left. In 1994, Republicans were favored by 59% of college graduates versus 34% favoring Democrats. In 2017, the numbers were 49% Democrat and 46% Republican.

LGBTQ Americans are an identity group for the Left and have moved left to their place next to African-Americans, Hispanics, and Feminists.

Women, who do not consider themselves Feminists, have been steadily moving to the left. Data gathered in 2017 shows 39% supporting the Democratic Party and 25% supporting the Republican Party.

The last category in the center is "think tanks". These organizations have become more numerous on the Right in response to the leftward move of academia. Conservative think tanks try to counter what they see as propaganda coming from academia and the mainstream media.

Given these shifts, more and more people are dissatisfied with politics and label themselves Independent. In 2017, 37% of those polled said they were not affiliated with one party. Those in the middle are not Tribalists because they understand nuanced points of view and don't believe every issue is black or white. The center chooses its positions based on logic and not ideology and is large enough to swing elections one way or the other. For more details on the trends discussed here see the Pew Research Center Study referenced below.[14]

------

[14] Pew Research Center, U.S. Politics and Policy. *Trends in Party Affiliation among Demographic Groups.* 2018

Academic

Academic disciplines that have embraced Postmodernism are now seriously degraded. Research output in these departments is dubious and emerges from a biased point of view. This one sidedness has leaked into American society through public sector institutions and the media.

The impact of Postmodernism is mainly concentrated in the Humanities and Social Sciences. The pure sciences rely on truth, so extreme positions questioning its existence do not gain much traction there. Art and architecture reflect Postmodernist ideas, but their own definitions, separate from Postmodernist philosophy. There are legitimate reasons for characterizing a period of art as Postmodernist, reflecting a period after Modernism, based on the evolution of art from a previous point in history, but that is different from disciplines that have absorbed Postmodernism into their theoretical foundation.

Postmodernism is the primary field of knowledge for education at the elite colleges of the United States. It is a strong component of about two dozen different disciplines, subfields, and areas of study, including Cultural Studies, Postcolonial Studies, Rhetoric and Composition, English

Literature, French Literature, American Studies, Film Studies, Women's Studies, Ethnic Studies, Queer Theory, Media Studies, Communications, Music Theory, Science and Technology Studies, Theater and Performance Studies, Anthropology, Continental Philosophy, and Theology.(ref) Even in the social sciences – in sociology, economics, geography, psychology, and political science – among those academics who identify with the emancipatory or 'critical' tradition, Postmodernism has begun to vie on at least equal ground with Marxism as the preferred ideology.[15]

The change in the role of knowledge in the university has altered the content of knowledge itself. Global competition for talent has turned universities into corporations that respond to market demands. The data shows that universities now hire more administrators than faculty, so they have become bloated bureaucracies.[16] Parts of that academic administrative apparatus is dedicated to policing the free expression of ideas and speech. Universities are also focused

---

[15] John Sanbonmatsu, John. 2006. *Postmodernism and The Corruption of The Academic Intelligentsia.* (Socialist Register, Volume 42, 2006), p. 4.

[16] Vedder, Richard. *"Kill all the Administrators" (Not really).* (Forbes online, May 10, 2018).

on marketing and providing first rate facilities to guarantee a good experience for the student, similar to the way hotel chains would operate.

Prior to about 1970, higher education was measured by the university's role to increase and expand human knowledge, build character in its students, and prepare them to become knowledgeable participants in modern society. Those mechanisms have been transformed in recent decades. The purpose of higher education today is to train workers who can excel when compared to peers in other countries.

In today's world, market pressure has increased the volume of humanities scholarships, while the quality of that work has degenerated. This benefits scholars who have the ability to market their work.

Traditional knowledge production, which was based on national security, is now tied to the interests of business. This has increased pressure on scholars in the Humanities and Social Sciences to find a business application for their subject area. Postmodernism with its revolutionary avant garde character is attractive to scholars seeking a new approach. This gives it sway in those disciplines. The

Humanities have been marketed as a tool for business analysis and innovation. Critical Theory, which was formerly used as justification for Socialist ideologies, was transformed into a tool to benefit the state. This integration of corporations, private foundations, intellectuals, and Postmodernism, with its ability to adapt to any ideological situation, has benefited from the new, corporate-like environment found in America's universities.

The second material factor in the university environment was the rise of the academic star system. The competition for resources launched a handful of academic scholars to the top of an increasingly inegalitarian and cutthroat Humanities system. These "stars" are not theorists, but practitioners of Postmodern orthodoxy. Their competitive environment fosters hostility toward all opposition, based on the availability of scarce academic resources. The Postmodern culture supports this environment through its attack on tradition and commonly accepted belief systems.

If the personal was political, then in the highly competitive world of academia, the personal was frequently also pathological. Today it's not uncommon for young academics to criticize the concept of democracy, questioning how such an unfair and corrupt idea could have had adherents during the Enlightenment. [17]

Research censorship

The impact of Tribalism on university faculty members has been profound and threatens the entire concept of intellectual research. Extremists on the Left have embraced identity issues and used them against all points of view that differ from their radical dogma.

For example, radical Feminists have attempted to push the idea that gender was culturally constructed, which is consistent with Postmodernist ideas. If true, that would suggest that women have been forced by men into roles they don't want; roles that need to be recast to allow women to achieve the freedom they seek. Researchers who produce data showing that men and women are different are attacked and accused of discrimination. This is a violation of the foundational concepts of academia that go back to the Middle Ages. Universities were supposed to be places where all ideas were freely expressed, no matter how controversial. Without opposing views, academia becomes an echo

---

[17] John Sanbonmatsu, 2006. Ibid.

chamber that corrupts itself. In today's academic climate, professors are afraid to do research when the results might be counter to the Left's ideology.

To offset this kind of pressure from the Left, it was recently announced that a new journal, the Journal of Controversial Ideas, will begin publication in 2019. This journal will allow academics to publish anonymously to avoid ridicule. The Left attacks this approach as dangerous, saying it will become a forum for the most radical views. It's hard to see that happening, however, given the fact that all papers published in the journal will be peer reviewed by experts in each field. The more logical explanation for the criticism is that the radicals see this journal as a threat to a narrative they wish to control.

Attack on Science

In a previous chapter, I stated that science has been immune from attacks of Postmodernists because of its obvious connection to reality based on the collection of empirical data. In reality, there was an attack on science during the 1990s by Postmodernists. This was the period of the "Science Wars," when a number of Postmodernists began reinterpreting science through the point of view of the scientist, rather than the discipline. Putting aside the results of the research, critics began looking for bias based on gender, sexual orientation, class, and race. In the book *Higher Superstition: The Academic Left and its Quarrels with Science,* Paul Gross and Norman Levitt accused the Postmodernists of anti-intellectualism and engaging in poor scholarship for political reasons. When attempts to mediate the differences between Science and Postmodernism in the late 1990s produced a standoff rather than a reconciliation, the Postmodernists moved on to something else.

It's appalling, in this Postmodern Age, that academics have to be concerned their research might offend the Left. This situation brings to mind the Inquisitions of the Middle Ages, like the trial of Galileo, where the famous astronomer was accused of heresy for supporting ideas different from those of the Catholic Church. It also recalls the Nazi book burnings, designed to control views that deviated from the Nazi belief system. The list of authors, whose books were burned, document the Nazi zeal for intellectual repression: Marx, Einstein, Freud, Heine, Kafka, Victor Hugo, Hemingway, Aldous Huxley, H.G. Wells, and Dostoyevsky. Has America become the 21st Century version of the Nazi suppression of the truth?

Students

Traditionally, universities have served as institutions where young people receive preparation for life in the real world. They selected a field of study and developed a deep knowledge in that subject in order to create the foundation for a successful career. Along the way, students were challenged by being exposed to opposing and controversial points of view so they could seek the truth for themselves.

Today's life in the university is the opposite. Students are encouraged to oppose authority and distrust traditional ideas. They are indoctrinated in identity politics and Postmodernism to gain an understanding of the evil of inequality and privilege. They protest against scheduled speakers (typically those on the Right), and shut down free speech. Statements like, "You have no right to speak, you're a white male," or "As a person who is in a position of power, your statements are suspect because your goal is to protect that power," or "The statistics you are presenting are questionable because they contradict the information, I was told is true."

For many students, Postmodernism was their primary exposure to critical thought. These students may not have had the benefit of exposure to alterative systems and are not shown papers critical of Postmodernist principles. That means the brightest of the middle and upper classes are being indoctrinated in a mode of discourse that is relativistic and skeptical. Many students are attracted by Postmodernism's playfulness and lack of respect for tradition. They come away believing they are involved in an important movement, when in fact they are being guided to a dead end.

The chart shown below demonstrates the Left bias in university faculties. They virtually guarantee that every student graduating has been exposed to Postmodern doctrine without hearing opposing points of view. Postmodernist ideas accelerate the drift to Tribalism because they introduce unwarranted bias in education and research. This is a direct assault on traditions that have served western society well for 200 years.

Distribution of Political affiliations in Universities

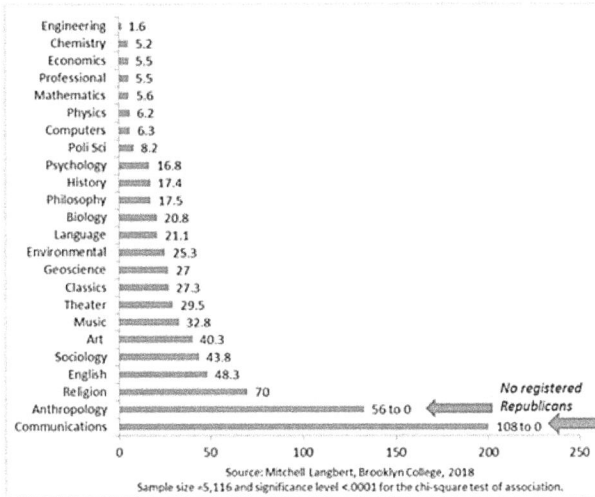

Discipline	Ratio
Engineering	1.6
Chemistry	5.2
Economics	5.5
Professional	5.5
Mathematics	5.6
Physics	6.2
Computers	6.3
Poli Sci	8.2
Psychology	16.8
History	17.4
Philosophy	17.5
Biology	20.8
Language	21.1
Environmental	25.3
Geoscience	27
Classics	27.3
Theater	29.5
Music	32.8
Art	40.3
Sociology	43.8
English	48.3
Religion	70
Anthropology	56 to 0 — No registered Republicans
Communications	108 to 0

Source: Mitchell Langbert, Brooklyn College, 2018
Sample size =5,116 and significance level <.0001 for the chi-square test of association.

This data was taken from a 2018 study of the political affiliation of university professors. For each of the 25 disciplines listed, there is a number indicating the ratio of Democrats to Republicans for each. Note that these are not absolute numbers, but ratios. For example, in Art there are 40 Democrat professors for each Republican professor. Two disciplines, Anthropology and Communications, had zero Republican professors.

The chart lays bare the degree of political bias that exists at elite universities.

Recent articles on the turmoil in Academia

Academics are well aware of the problems in their institutions. The following are some recent quotes in the subject.

Debra Soh. 2018. *Can Academia be Saved from the Mob?* @DebraSoh, December 4, 2018. "The culture of fear and intimidation academics face impedes academic freedom and the ability to conduct meaningful work..."

Lindsay, James A. 2018. *Are Academics Cowards? The Grip of Grievance Studies and the Sunk Costs of Academic Pursuit.* Areo Digital Magazine, December 4, 2018. "There is much that should be said about the ways in which the dominant Social Justice ideology has negative impacts upon the university, free expression, academic freedom and, especially, the sciences..."

Berkman, Eliot. 2018. *The Self-Defeat of Academia.* Quillette, August 27, 2018. "These last few years have been tough for higher education. Enrollment is down year after year, state funding increases have stalled even as costs skyrocket, and most people don't have much confidence overall in American colleges and universities..."

Goldstein, Evan. 2018. *Jill Lepore on writing the story of America, the rise and fall of the fact, and how women's intellectual authority is undermined.* Interview in The Chronicle of Higher Education. November 13, 2018. "When people talk about the decline of the humanities, they are actually talking about the rise and fall of the fact, as well as other factors... Academia is largely itself responsible for its own peril. The retreat of humanists from public life has had enormous consequences for the prestige of humanistic ways of knowing and understanding the world..."

Impact on the American Public

What damage has Tribalism done to the American public and how do we measure it? We get some answers from a study performed by the group *More in Common* and published in 2018.[18] This study gathered questionnaires from nearly 8,000 people. Its goal was to identify the core beliefs of individual Americans, including moral values, social values, and political ideology. Cluster analysis was applied to the data to identify possible grouping trends and the analysis showed that seven different factions that make

---

[18] Stephen **Hawkins, Daniel Yudkin, Miriam Juan-Torres, and Tim Dixon**. *Hidden Tribes: A Study of America's Polarized Landscape*. (Publisher - More in Common, 2018)

up the American electorate -- Progressive Activists, Traditional Liberals, Passive Liberals, Politically Disengaged, Moderates, Traditional Conservatives, and Devoted Conservatives.

The factions themselves are not relevant to the discussion here, but the data offers a window into the way Americans view Tribalism. Each faction has a different type of response, based on their political morality and station in life.

Progressive activists (8% of the population) are eighty percent white and likely have college degrees. They feel secure about themselves, most likely because they don't have money problems. They have an aggressive approach to correcting the defects they see in American society, based on a high sensitivity to fairness and equality. They don't mention Tribalism as a concern perhaps because they understand achieving social justice is difficult and controversial.

Traditional Liberals (11% of the population), are seventy-six percent white and likely have a college education. They reflect the liberal views of the Baby Boomer generation and support social justice with less enthusiasm than Progressive

Activists do. Traditional Liberals observe Tribalism and believe its solution lies in America healing as a nation through tolerance of different points of view and compromise where necessary. Seventy-five percent say freedom and equality are important to them.

Passive Liberals (15% of the population), are only weakly engaged in politics, but have a modern view of social issues when pushed to state their positions. This group feels isolated and alienated from their community. Seventy-two percent are not registered to vote and two-thirds do not have a college degree. They generally believe events in their lives are outside of their control. Fifty percent say the world is becoming a more dangerous place. Fifty-nine percent are female. Eighty-six percent try to avoid situations where there could be arguments.

The Politically Disengaged (26% of the population), tend to be lower income and are not engaged in politics. Forty-one percent make less than $ 30,000 per year. They are more anxious than Passive Liberals about external threats and are reluctant to discuss differences with others. They are extremely pessimistic about resolving Tribalism. Thirty-two percent say that the differences between Americans are too big to resolve.

Moderates (15% of the population), represent the political middle of the road. They are involved in their communities, volunteer, and are engaged in current affairs. This group is very troubled by Tribalism. Moderates dislike the extremism that exists at both ends of the political spectrum. They feel the American identity is slipping away. Eighty-nine percent feel that political correctness has gone too far. Sixty percent are over 45.

Traditional Conservatives (19% of the population), feel that America's foundations are under attack from a liberal political culture that emphasizes diversity and downplays American accomplishments. Seventy-nine percent are white. Only forty-seven percent say America is rigged to favor the rich. Traditional Conservatives are open to discussing bipartisan solutions to America's problems.

Devoted Conservatives (6% of the population), are the equivalent of the Progressive Activists at the other end of the political spectrum. Like their cousins, they are happy and secure in life. They see American traditions under assault and feel forced to accept Liberal dogma. This group is 88% white, 34% over 65 years of age, and 63% opposed to compromise on traditional values.

The attitudes uncovered in this study demonstrate the American people's concerns about Tribalism. Nearly two-thirds of the respondents fall into groups that are worried about the country. The other third sits at the ends of the political spectrum. For those groups, it would appear that the pursuit of ideological goals outweighs concerns over collateral damage.

POINTS TO REMEMBER

- Damage caused by Tribalism in America is strongly evident in the political sphere, where the parties grow farther and father apart. This phenomenon can be observed in the groups that support each party and their migration from the center. The result of division is ineffective government resulting from an unwillingness to compromise.

- Academia has been damaged by the corruption of its mission by Postmodernism. That fact is evident by observing the way universities operate, their path toward ideological exclusion, and the impact they have on students.

- The American people, as a whole, are affected by Tribalism; psychologically through its impact on their beliefs about our country and socially in the way it impacts relationships with others. Groups that are pessimistic, by nature, see Tribalism as just one more scary element in life.

CHAPTER TWELVE

A PERSPECTIVE ON AMERICAN TRIBALISM

In history, a great volume is unrolled for our instruction, drawing the materials of future wisdom from the past errors and infirmities of mankind. **Edmund Burke**

For many reasons, the current Tribal state in America is unhealthy for our culture. The country is divided, with no prospect of compromise, because the level of vitriol prevents dialog between the tribes. Politics are adversarial and that impacts the operation of our government, preventing meaningful progress on either side of the aisle. Is this crisis a unique phenomenon or something that has appeared before in history?

History has always been a place to learn. Historical events can be a guide to the present, even when the similarity is imperfect. Human society is 7000 years old and across that time frame political systems have served as a laboratory for human behavior in large groups. Large societies produce forces that aggregate and develop momentum for good or bad. Sometimes man is able to fix the problems he causes. Sometimes the problems evolve beyond human control.

Throughout history, human beings have tried to find ways to achieve a satisfying life. Their motivations are summarized in Maslow's hierarchy of needs. People may differ in what they want out of life, but all must take care of the basic human needs, to be safe, and to live comfortably in human society.

Maslow's hierarchy can be divided into three groups: material needs, social needs, and spiritual needs. Material needs are physiological; social needs are based upon a sense of belonging to a group; and spiritual needs are met through a connection that goes beyond the self.

Self-Actualization
realizing personal potential

Esteem needs
prestige and feeling of accomplishment

Belonging and love needs
intimate relationships, friends

Safety needs
security, safety

Physiological needs
water, warmth, rest

As social animals, human beings seek social relationships as a fundamental component of life. The ability to interact with friends and seeking the love and companionship of a partner are a part of being human. Human society promotes a specific morality based on the common beliefs of its members, so man will embrace his society when it offers more than a tribe can. When society fails to provide for human needs, man reverts to tribal ways.

Analogs to American Tribalism
Finding analogs for the current Tribalist state of America is challenging. The United States today is an expanding multicultural society with several identity groups. Each group has gravitated to the Left or the Right, leaving few links between the tribes. In history, particularly ancient

history, multiculturalism was not common and identity groups had no standing. Most groups lacked representation because of legal barriers or cultural norms. For example, in the Roman Republic (and Empire), only Roman citizens had standing. All other groups, even the Italian people living near Rome, were not guaranteed the benefits of Roman citizenship. Women, children, and slaves had no standing and were considered the property of men.

In the barbarian world, ethnic groups were organized into competing tribes allied with or fought against other tribes. These were no sovereign states and had no government, so there was no motivation to address the interests of minority groups.

Tribalism in the Roman Republic

There are many similarities between the government of the Roman Republic and the American political system. Rome served as the model the American founders used to create our government; two branches in the legislature and a chief magistrate or executive being the main components. The United States is a republic of republics; a republican federal government and its republican states. Its founders knew that the Greek democracy could not work in North America and they saw the Roman model as a better fit for the new nation.

As history has documented, the Roman Republic fell and became an authoritarian dictatorship. There are many factors that precipitated the fall, not the least of which was Tribalism. Rome had no formal political parties, but in the period after 140 BC, two political factions came into being and helped create instability in the Republic; a conservative faction supporting the Senate and a liberal faction supporting the interests of the people.

The Roman Senate and Assembly acted together as the legislative body of the Republic. The Senate had enormous power and was made up of the richest and most influential Romans. The Assembly was made up of the common people (Plebeians). The Assembly voted on new laws and elected magistrates for government service. The Senate introduced new candidates and bills but had no power over the election process, other than behind the scenes coercion. The Assembly was presided over by the college of Tribunes: ten magistrates elected by the Plebeians.

In 133 BC, a dispute arose over the passage of a land bill designed to lift Romans out of poverty. The makeup of the Roman citizen army had created this problem. To serve in the army, a man had to own property, so most soldiers were farmers. When they died in battle, their families were left with no head of household and had difficulty maintaining their farms. Many properties had to be sold and farm workers were displaced. Over time, more and more families were forced to migrate to Rome to find work. A high death rate also meant the army was short of recruits, so it made sense to encourage the formation of new farms whose owners could serve in the army.

We see this same behavior in the history of the United States. Pioneers traveled west in search of a better life, a life they could control. In the periods when the United Sates was transitioning from a rural farming-based economy to an urban industrial economy, its people migrated to cities, where the opportunity to find work seemed brightest.

The leader of the tribunes, in 133 BC, was Tiberius Gracchus, an independent thinker with a solid Roman pedigree based on his family's history of serving the Republic. Gracchus pushed a land bill through the assembly that would provide free land to those who were willing to set up farms on their land. The property was to be taken from the *Ager Publicus*: land owned by the Roman people jointly and administered by the Senate.

Tiberius' land bill caused a great controversy because wealthy Senators were using the *Ager Publicus* for their own purposes and enriching themselves. They did not want to give up land they controlled for startup farms. The Senate did all it could to stop implementation of the new law, delaying votes on the bill for the entire year of Tiberius' term of office. He decided to run for a second term to complete the land redeployment project, even though second terms were unprecedented for tribunes. This decision aroused the Senate against him. On the day of the election, agents of the Senate induced a riot, and Tiberius was assassinated. As a result of this incident, a new political faction called the "Populares" arose among the Plebeians; these were men who were sympathetic to the goals of Tiberius and wanted to see the problems of the poor resolved. The Senate countered with its own faction, the "Optimates" (best men). The two factions grew and adopted a tribal attitude toward each other. In 122 BC, Tiberius' younger brother Gaius was elected tribune and planned to finish the work of his brother.

Unfortunately, like, his brother, Gaius was elected to a second term and then assassinated.

The Senate was now permanently stained because the public knew they were behind the assassinations of the Gracchus brothers. This empowered the populares to seek more power for the people and strip away the power of the Senate. In 107 BC, a Plebeian general, Marius, ran for consul on the platform that he could end a war in Africa which had been dragging on for years. Marius had enemies in the Senate who sought to block him but Marius' status as a Populare and public outcry against the Senate prompted the Assembly to name him commander of the African campaign. Marius was victorious and the people were emboldened by their new found power.

As time passed, there was no way the Tribalism between the Optimates and the Populares could be resolved. The Plebeians were on a permanent path toward stripping the power of the Senate and ending its protection of the wealthy class.

Based on his appeals to the Populare faction, Julius Caesar was able to implement the land bill introduced by the

Gracchus brothers seventy-five years earlier. Caesar's motive was to use the Populares for his own political advancement. His goal, of course, was to become Emperor of Rome. Although he was only in power for five years, Caesar started Rome down the path toward an Empire. There already were cracks in the system which Caesar helped worsen, causing the Republic to fall apart. The political factions of Populares and Optimates were swept away with the rest of the old government.

This Tribalism in Rome was never resolved because it went to the heart of class and power. The Plebeians were willing to fight against the Senate for equal rights and the corruption of the Senate, based on its desire to hold onto power, ultimately became its weakness.

Religious tribalism in Medieval Europe

The great religious disruption in Europe, starting in the early 16th Century and extending for nearly two hundred years, stands as one of the most important examples of Tribalism in the history of Western Civilization. The tribes were Catholic and Protestant initially, fighting over perceived corruption of the Catholic Church and the need to reform it. Europe's power brokers used the situation to advance their influence and take power away from the Vatican. It was the leaders who were tribal; not the people. The people were caught in the middle and suffered for it.

The low point in this era of tribal pain was the Thirty Years War (1618-1648), which directly led to the deaths of eight million people (mostly German), from disease, famine, and battle. Tribal conflict ended with the stroke of a pen at the Treaty of Westphalia in 1648, which launched the nation state and changed Europe forever.

For 500 years, the Holy Roman Empire had linked together a large portion of central Europe. It was, in practice, a weakly governed collection of independent states including large kingdoms like the House of Habsburg, regional powers like the Duchy of Bavaria, free cities, and petty lordships as small as a single village. The Holy Roman Emperor was an elected official and served as titular head of this Empire. His lack of authority and the large number of client states was an admixture that would foster Tribalism, once the tribes were defined. Prior to 1517, there was only one religious tribe; the Catholics. No other religions were sanctioned by the empires of Europe.

Martin Luther was the antagonist who set the tribal wheels in motion. Luther's publication of his 95 treatises, in 1517, represented a direct attack on the Catholic Church for abuses Luther could not tolerate. His refusal to disavow these criticisms led to his excommunication by the Vatican. By 1526, Luther had begun the founding of a new church. This new faith was quickly embraced by some of the powerful, as a way to transfer power from the Vatican to themselves. Others, seeing Luther's attack on their Catholic faith, became crusaders for Rome. As early as 1545, the new Protestant tribe found itself at war with the German Catholics over religious control of Protestant territory. The war ended in 1555 with the Peace of Augsburg, which gave the states of the Holy Roman Empire the right to choose their own religion. The term "cuius regio, eius religio", one of the terms of the treaty, means *his realm, his religion.*

The peace of Augsburg did not solve the underlying problems in the empire because it only addressed Catholic-Lutheran concerns and ignored the burgeoning Calvinist faith. Moreover, it did not settle the growing antagonism between powerful states who not only were dogmatic about their religion, but also were willing to go to war to advance the cause of their faith.

Spain was interested in the German states because they held certain territory affiliated with them. The southern portion of the Netherlands was under the control of Spain and revolted in the 1560s, seeking independence. France found itself between the Western Hapsburg Empire in Spain and the Holy Roman Empire to its east, feeling threatened from both sides. To the north, Sweden and Denmark sought control over the northern German states that bordered on the Baltic Sea in order to protect their Protestant and political interests. From the top, it was a game of using religion as a tool to hold or expand power. At the bottom of society, it was only the desire for religious expression that mattered to the people.

During the second half of the 16th Century, the Peace of Augsburg began to unravel. Some bishops refused to abandon their dioceses even though they had chosen to become Protestant. Spain, anxious to act on behalf of the Pope, looked for an opportunity to restore Catholicism across the Holy Roman Empire. When the prince-archbishop of the city of Cologne converted to Calvinism, it opened the door for the election of a Protestant Holy Roman Emperor. This had never happened previously. Spain, representing Vatican interests, sent troops to Cologne in 1583, and replaced the elector archbishop with a Catholic.

By the turn of the 17th Century, the Rhine lands and areas south of the Danube were largely Catholic, Lutherans predominated in the north, and Calvinists filled in various pockets in between.

Violence broke out in 1606 when a Lutheran majority prohibited a Catholic festival in the town of Donauworth. The subsequent riots were suppressed via the intervention of the Duke of Bavaria, a Catholic. The Calvinists, who felt the most threatened, banded together to form the Protestant League. In response, the Catholics formed their own league in 1609.

Bohemian Revolt (1618-1625)

In 1617, Matthias, the Holy Roman Emperor and King of Bohemia, died without an heir and Archduke Ferdinand of Austria became emperor. Ferdinand was a devout Catholic, who wanted to impose religious uniformity on the empire, reversing a more lenient approach taken by Matthias. When Ferdinand sent representatives to Prague to take over the government in his absence, they were thrown out of the palace window by a group of Protestants in what came to be known as the Second Defenestration of Prague. This single event was the tipping point that launched the Thirty Years

War.

Bohemian Protestants applied to become members of the Protestant League and elected their own king, Frederick V elector of the Palatinate area of the Rhine. They also received support from Upper Austria, the English, Scots, and the Dutch for their cause. Despite having a sizable army, the Protestants were defeated by the Imperial forces, allied with a Spanish Army, at the Battle of White Mountain in 1620, causing the collapse of the Protestant League. This phase of the war continued when the Protestant prince of Transylvania, allied with the Ottoman Turks, attacked Poland in support of Bohemia. After several battles the Poles were able to recover and the prince withdrew. After the Polish conflict ended in 1621, the war continued in the Palatinate, which included states along the Rhine River in Germany. The imperial forces battled the remnants of the Protestant army and, by 1625, utterly defeated them, and drove Frederick into exile.

Intervention from the North (1625-35)

In 1625, the Danish king, Christian IV, led an attack against imperial forces in order to protect his sovereignty against the growing power of the Catholics. His army was partly subsidized by the king of France, his uncle. Christian was opposed by the imperial emperor's commander, Albrecht von Wallenstein, a Bohemian nobleman. The Catholic army pushed Christian all the way back to Copenhagen, before his army was finally able to halt the Catholic advance. A truce was followed by the Treaty at Lubeck (1629), which allowed Christian to keep Denmark-Norway in return for withdrawing his support for the Protestants.

Wallenstein's behavior against the Danes was a warning to his superiors. He did not obey orders and began to poach soldiers from his Catholic allies, causing them protest that Wallenstein was out of control. Ferdinand ignored these complaints because he had a master plan to recover all the Catholic lands previously taken by the Protestants, and needed Wallenstein as his sword. Ferdinand was on his way to defeating the Protestants for good when his cousin, the king of Spain caused a distraction that destroyed his chances for success. Philip asked Ferdinand to attack the Duchy of Mantua in Italy, which was held by his enemy the French. That intervention angered the Pope, who was a friend of Mantua. The resulting break between Ferdinand and Rome split the Catholics and kept the war going for another eighteen years.

Now came the time for King Gustavus Adolphus of Sweden to take his turn. Gustavus' goal was to protect Swedish territorial interests and block the Catholics from overrunning Lutheran territory. He looked forward to the support of the French and the Dutch in that effort. While the Catholics fought amongst themselves, the king of Sweden began his invasion of the territories adjacent to the Baltic Sea. Gustavus began his campaign in Pomerania, which was on the Baltic coast, split between Germany and Poland. Successful there, he won the Battle of Breitenfeld in 1631. Following a string of victories, Gustavus was killed at the Battle of Lutzen in late 1632, although the Swedish army was victorious.

Control of Northern Germany became a battle between diplomats: Gustavus' second-in- command Oxenstierna and King Ferdinand, the Holy Roman Emperor. The French were duplicitous and played both sides. The war continued and the Swedish army was beaten decisively at the battle of Nordlingen in 1634. A temporary peace was achieved in 1635 at the Peace of Prague, where an agreement was reached between the Holy Roman Emperor and the German states. The emperor agreed to halt the confiscation of

Protestant lands for 40 years, which had the effect of protecting the Lutheran cause in Northern Germany.

Left out of the treaty, the Swedes continued the war for another nine years, joined by France who declared war on the empire. France's participation produced mixed results for them; mainly alternating victories against the Spanish army. The Swedes were successful enough in their German campaigns to convince the new emperor, Ferdinand III, that they would have to be part of any treaty discussion.

Final negotiations to end the Thirty Years War began in 1644 and progressed over a four-year span. Treaties were signed in the cities of Munster and Osnabruck because many of the participants insisted on negotiating in a location, thought to be safe for them. The Treaty of Munster contained agreements between the Holy Roman Empire and France. The Treaty of Osnabruck was between the Holy Roman Empire and Sweden. These treaties reduced the power of the Holy Roman Emperor and transferred that power back to the German states. All states were allowed to choose their own official religion between Catholic, Protestant, and Calvinism. Citizens could practice their own religion, if different from the state's official religion as long as they did so in private. Pope Innocent X was extremely displeased by the treaties and condemned them.

The treaties set a precedent for European diplomacy, allowing ambassadors and negotiators to act on the behalf of their kings. More importantly, they established the inviolability of state borders and the idea that one state had no right to interfere in another state's internal matters. Religious Tribalism ended once and for all in Europe, with the adoption of the Westphalian treaties. Catholicism, Protestantism, and Calvinism were established as equals, ending religion as an excuse for war.

Tribalism in American History

America's first tribes were religious. It was the early 17th Century when settlers came to New England from Europe to escape persecution. This was before the time of the Enlightenment, when religious persecution was at its most extreme in Europe. Although these groups were persecuted in Europe, they became intolerant themselves after arriving in North America. Severe penalties, including execution, were enforced by the Massachusetts Bay Colony against anyone who did not follow the Puritan religion. Religious extremism became less common over time, as an expanding number of religions became established in the colonies and religious toleration in Europe was evangelized.

Quakers were early settlers in Rhode Island and then prospered in Pennsylvania under William Penn. Maryland was settled by Catholics. Virginia, the largest colony, was a focus of the Church of England which had sent 22 priests to the colony by 1624. The South, during the late Colonial period, saw the Baptist and Methodist religions expand across its geography. By the time of the Revolution, all colonies enjoyed a variety of religious denominations and tolerance was universal. Religious Tribalism in the colonies lasted about 30 years and ended when religious groups lost their ability to use government to control the beliefs of the people.

Slavery

The second great tribal confrontation in America involved slavery. The tribes were the pro-slavery Southern states and the anti-slavery Northern states. Slavery was an essential component of the Southern economy; its importance to the South stimulated a vigorous debate at the Constitutional Convention. Early on, it was obvious to the delegates from the North that the South would never become part of a

Federal government that had anti-slavery provisions written into its Constitution. With elimination of slavery off the table, debate was reduced to two issues; counting slaves for the purpose of representation and eliminating slave trade.

The central problem of representation was how the slaves would be counted. Were they property or not? If they were property, they should not be counted for representation. If they weren't property, what was their designation? The Southern states wanted slaves to be counted one for one because that would swell their populations and give them a larger representation. The Northern states had the opposite view. In the end, a compromise was negotiated so that three-fifths of the slaves would be counted for representation.

As an initial step toward ending slavery, the delegates from the North wanted a concession that would limit the importation of slaves to America. After some strenuous negotiations, an agreement was reached that 20 years after the Constitution was ratified, importing of slaves would be outlawed in the United States. Both sides received something in the bargain. The North was able to put a cap on the growth of slavery and the South was able to avoid economic disruption because of a change of status of slaves.

The tribes understood this was a minor step, which prolonged the problem of slavery rather than solving it. The parties must have known that civil war was inevitable.

The primary factors that precipitated the war were the South's growing concern that the forces against slavery would increase to a point of no return. First, new states were being added to the Union that were designated free states. With each free state added, the ratio of free to slave states increased, putting the South in a weaker position. Second, the South felt that the federal government was violating states' rights and overstepping the Constitution by pursuing an anti-slavery agenda. In other words, the federal government was representing the North instead of the whole country.

After Lincoln's election on November 6, 1860, the South prepared to leave the Union. South Carolina was the first state to secede on December 20th 1860. The Civil War began with the attack on Fort Sumter in April of 1861. Before it ended in 1865, some 600,000 Americans had been killed. The Tribal confrontation over slavery lasted seventy-five years from the ratification of the Constitution until the end of the Civil War. It ended abruptly, but not before an enormous price had been paid.

The Progressive Movement

The third great Tribal confrontation in American history began in the 1880s when horrible working conditions in the American industry and political corruption in American cities became so offensive to the American people, they demanded change. The common people united as one tribe to oppose what they saw as an unfair and corrupt status quo. The corrupt politicians and robber barons fought back in order to retain their advantage.

Workers began to form unions to agitate for better pay and working conditions. Socialist ideas were imported from Europe and new socialist organization began to attack Capitalism. Women began their fight for the right to vote. Religious groups united to form the Anti-Saloon League for the purpose of eliminating the sale and consumption of alcohol. There was universal agitation for better working conditions and fewer hours in the work week.

Corruption in city politics was curtailed through increasing the authority of urban government. This helped eliminate the "boss" system in which local political power brokers bribed their state governments in exchange for local contracts that would enrich them. Cities were permitted to collect their own fees and taxes so they wouldn't be dependent on the states for funding.

Theodore Roosevelt, elected in 1904, was one of America's greatest Progressives, advocating for the control of big corporations and protection of the environment. When Roosevelt chose not to run in 1908, the Progressive Movement began to migrate to the Democratic Party. The Movement diminished in importance during the war years and the Roaring Twenties, because the country was distracted. Still, it had raised awareness about social justice and forced the Federal government to pass laws needed to protect the people. This 35-year Tribal period ended when the winning Tribe was able to achieve its major goals.

Today we are in the midst of America's fourth great Tribal battle. How will it be resolved? The first one ended by the Constitutional separation of church and state, the second by war, and the third by changing the role of the Federal government in ways that would protect the people.

These examples of Tribalism represent analogues to what we experience in America today. They have been included as illustrations of the forms Tribalism can take and how long it can last. The United States is in the second decade of its tribal experience. How many decades this condition will continue is unknown.

POINTS TO REMEMBER

- There are points in history that give us clues about Tribalism and how it behaves.

- Two examples involve the faction wars of the Roman Republic and the religious wars prior to the Enlightenment.

- America has experienced its own Tribal conflicts in the past, including battles over intolerant religious practices, slavery, and exploitation of the common man.

- Every Tribal experience has its own characteristics making its outcome unpredictable.

CHAPTER THIRTEEN

MORAL CAPITAL

Moral Capital is the glue that holds a society together, for good or bad. **Unknown**

We described in Chapter Twelve, how Tribalism has impacted academia, politics, and the American people. Overtime, as academia moved toward Postmodernism and migrated to the Left, its influence reached the political sphere and then the people. Politics is a mirror of the American society adapting to what it thinks the people want, but politics can also divide when it becomes polarized. Our society has experienced enormous changes in the past fifty years and those changes have created an unsettling feeling in the minds of Americans. Postmodernists tell us that unsettling feeling is an indicator we are in a new world and have to think differently. To do that, we have to discard the stability we experienced in the Modern Age.

To think about this problem another way, consider American society as a unit: as three hundred million people living in a fixed geography, each subject to the laws and policies of their state and Federal government. In any society, there are forces that influence its stability; political forces, economic forces, and social forces They can foster stability, or they can breed uncertainty and discontent. One way to measure stability is to look at the amount of Moral Capital it possesses.

The word "capital," meaning to provide value, is used in several different but related forms. Capital is surplus value in an economic system. When a business makes a profit, it is creating capital. Similarly, political capital is value earned that allows a political idea to move forward. A newly elected President has an excess of political capital in the first year of his presidency because he has been given a mandate by the American people and has earned the chance to implement the programs that got him elected. A related term is "social capital," which refers to the interconnectivity of people in a society. That interconnectivity comes from relationships that are marked by reciprocity, trust, and cooperation.

For our purposes here, moral capital is the amount of moral connectivity that exists in a society. The term originally appeared in Jonathan Haidt's *The Righteous Mind*. Haidt wrote:

Moral Capital refers to the degree to which a community possesses interlocking sets of values, virtues, norms, practices, identities, institutions, and technologies that mesh well with evolved psychological mechanisms and thereby enable the community to suppress or regulate selfishness and make cooperation possible.[19]

Social capital measures how the interaction between people can generate efficiency and connectivity. Moral capital goes one level deeper; it describes connectivity with a moral value

---

[19] Jonathan Haidt. *The Righteous Mind, Why Good People are divided by Politics and Religion.* (New York: Pantheon Books, 2012) p. 270.

attached to it. People who are socially connected communicate in ways that foster the sharing of opinions and ideas. People who are morally connected share a kinship based on common beliefs and satisfaction from belonging and sharing experiences. As we discussed in Chapter Twelve, human beings want to find their place on Maslow's Hierarchy of Needs. A sense of belonging, a shared set of beliefs, and self-actualization are contributors to Moral capital.

I suggest that there are four types of moral capital: family, local community, moral community, and nationalism or patriotism.

Family

The family is the most fundamental human grouping, as old as man himself. The moral value of family is the shared experience of life and the protection provided by family members. Men and women live together and share the task of raising the children they produce. The relationships within family have the strongest moral capital because they form the closest personal relationships between and among human beings. Those relationships last a lifetime. When all things crash in a person's life, the family serves as a backstop to offer support. Because the family is the most important personal connection in human life, it has the most devastating impact when it fails. Broken marriages, domestic violence, and psycho-emotional abuse create real and invisible scars that may surpass a lifetime, and continue for generations.

Local Community

Local community is defined by the relationships among friends, neighbors, and co-workers. Individuals are most often interacting with their local community when they are not with their family. Local community provides the security of social interaction with others who live and work in the same space. Its moral value is shared experiences and self-actualization through work relationships.

Moral Community

Moral communities are built through participation in any system of faith, belief, or worship. The category goes beyond religion because there are moral communities that are not religious. The moral value is socialization, a sense of belonging, and the feeling of being part of something important. It exists in organizations that have altruistic objectives and deliver services to those who need them.

Religions bring together people who share the same belief system. Their connection follows from community worship service to activities where individuals contribute time for the benefit of others. Non-religious moral communities are also based on common belief systems. Organizations like the Rotary Club have a set of standards and public service goals that are required for members. The act of pursuing those goals builds a stronger connection within the group.

Loyalty to sports teams is another type of moral community. Americans are fanatically involved in sports and each team in each city has its own tribe of followers. Surveys have shown that 70% of Millennials are sports fans. A city's fanbase is a moral community because it goes beyond the social community that's part of attending a game. Fans create a family-like atmosphere around their team, worshiping their heroes and carrying the pain of defeat in the hope of future victories.

Sports behavior is an acceptable application of Tribalism because it is non-confrontational and fans understand the point of view of opposition fans. There is an unwritten rule to respect the opponent's fan in the next seat, you want him to lose, but you're not going to start an argument over his choice of teams.

Patriotism

The broadest of the elements of moral capital is loyalty to country. Patriotism is the glue that unites a nation and allows it to endure its greatest challenges and mark its greatest collective triumphs. Patriotism and love of country connect every ethnic, cultural, social, and political group. Its moral value is a shared culture and a common way of life to protect. Threats to a nation are threats to all its people and can galvanize a society into unity of purpose. Moral capital, based on national interests, is the most fragile of the types because it's impersonal. It is not derived from relationships between individuals, but rather from a perceived connection to fellow citizens based on language, geography, and nationality.

Moral Capital in Operation

Social stability depends on the amount of moral capital in the society. It must be rebuilt when its degraded or the society becomes unstable. If it is not, the society becomes Tribal. When we think about national unity as a contributor to moral capital, the challenge is enormous, and the threat of discontinuity is great. If a person loses pride in his nation, he won't support the values, virtues, and norms that are a part of the national fabric.

Moral capital is not universally good. There is a risk it might be harnessed for evil purposes. All would agree that the Nazi regime was immoral. During the time the Nazis were gaining popularity, Germany saw a rise in economic capital, social capital, and moral capital. Its moral capital was based on unity, gained from the character and traditions of the German people. This reinforced a belief in the superiority of the German nation. Unfortunately, the Nazi regime perverted the use of moral capital in ways that were hidden from the German people until it was too late. They became captive to an ideology bent on world conquest and genocide. The same ideology that harnessed moral capital to unite the German nation, almost destroyed it.

Consider the example of the Soviet Union. What started out to be a political system intent on implementing Marxian ideology, produced a despotic dictatorship instead. Moral capital was invented by the regime for propaganda purposes and did not reflect the true feelings of the Russian people. When it was needed to hold the regime together at the end of the 1980s, moral capital showed itself to be an illusion, and the authoritarian structure collapsed.

The United States has always aspired to be a society with moral capital. At the time of its founding, the dreams of the nation's founders were distilled from the moral capital of its people and placed in the Constitution.

Religion was a strong component of America's moral capital from the beginning. Many of the first settlers were seeking to escape from religious persecution in Europe and hoped to find religious freedom in America. They came as families and family was the fundamental unit of colonial settlements. Often the settlers came in groups of multiple families, because they were members of the same neighborhood or parish in the old country. Colonial towns were small, and neighbors served together as members of town councils. America remained a population of small towns until well beyond the time of the Constitution. In 1790, there were only five cities with populations greater than 10,000. By 1810, there were ten. By 1840, there were three cities with more than 100,000 inhabitants. This shows how family and community were able to generate and retain moral capital. People's lives were local, they knew everyone in their community, and they shared common values with their friends. They were tribe-like in the sense that family, community, and church were intertwined in the same social group.

At the time of the Revolutionary War, America was divided by loyalty to the Crown and loyalty to the new nation. Moral capital, based on patriotism, did not show up until the country became larger and communication improved. America's strength as a nation emerged at the end of World War I when it first stepped onto the world stage. Our engagement in the Great War was late and we only played a minor role, but America showed it was committed to defending the beliefs of the West. When Pearl Harbor was attacked in 1941, our moral capital reached a peak, as all Americans became brothers and sisters united to destroy those who had attacked us.

Patriotism has ebbs and flows depending on unity generated by threats from the outside. If there is disagreement about the extent of those threats, as in the case of the Viet Nam War, moral capital is degraded rather than enhanced. Its value also depends on the degree of unity about the role of our government. If people are divided about the priorities of government, moral capital is reduced. As much as we'd like to keep moral capital at a high level, it's a lot harder in doing than in wishing it were so. Changing human society often moves toward disunity because of the political, economic, and social forces placed on it. Decades may pass before a society becomes unified again.

The Decline in Moral Capital

Most Americans would say they feel a sense of unease over changes in our society over the last decades. That unease has been a contributor to Tribalism. What is it that has changed and how have those changes influenced us? Robert Putnam's book *Bowling Alone* provides us with help in answering those questions. Putnam's objective, in writing his book, was to look for reasons why there has been a breakdown in community across the United States between the years 1960-2000. He gathered voluminous data on the changes in American social behavior and used the data to speculate on the drivers for social change.

The American family has changed radically. Divorce rates increased in the last decades of the 20th Century and there were more single parents raising children. Single mothers have a difficult time juggling work and child care, which often leads them into poverty. About 20% of children lived with a solo parent in 2017. Men and women are getting married later (averaging about 28 years old) or cohabitating (8.5 million in 2018) and are not married. Another 35 million live in single person households, making up 28% of all households. Thirty-two percent of adults over 15 years old have never been married. Marriage has been redefined and no longer refers only to a union between a man and a woman.

Changes in the local community have mainly come from changes in the family and the pace of life. Families have less time and money, and that has a direct impact on social engagement. Children get transported by parents to their many activities, which takes time. Parents' fear of harm to their children translates into constant supervision. Movement from the city to the suburbs has spread people out, breaking up old neighborhood relationships. Television and the Internet have become stay at home entertainment platforms which substitute for social relationships. Social club membership dropped significantly from 1960 to 2000.

Moral community involvement has waned. Religious participation dropped 10% between 1960 and 2000.

Meanwhile the percentage of people claiming to be unreligious has quadrupled.

Putnam estimated that the contributors to the decrease in human socialization in the United States were; lack of time or money 10%, suburbanization 10%, Television 25%, with generational changes making up the remaining 50%. The latter refers to natural changes in behavior that occur from one generation to the next. The generations after the Baby Boomers are not as interested in social interaction as their predecessors were.

As every American can sense, Patriotism and pride in country are down from previous levels. This metric measures the harmony among the American people, and the degree of unity about the direction the country should take. The last time that number was above 50% was 2005, so we are in a 14-year cycle of dissatisfaction with our government.

Putnam engages in an interesting discussion he calls "the dark side of social capital." A study of group behavior in the United States makes it apparent that fraternity (a state of feeling like someone belongs to a group that shares their interests), equality, and liberty are forces in tension. In the past 40 years, as community participation has decreased, social equality (as measured by tolerance) has increased. Americans are more tolerant than they used to be of those who behave differently than they do. This is probably related to the trend toward political correctness which is a drive toward equality. Loss of community also reflects a growth in individual freedom. This is the outcome of the Enlightenment, reborn. Interestingly, in today's environment, the most intolerant groups (e.g. neo-Nazis), are the least connected to society.

It is important to point out that America's growing economic inequality is a fundamental contributor to the loss of moral capital. Those disenfranchised Americans who are sinking into financial trouble exhibit a greater loss of moral capital than the rest of the population. This encompasses money pressure from intermittent work or unemployment and stress because of the difficulty of maintaining a lifestyle. There is less community involvement, less engagement in moral communities, and a disinterest in politics. As we discussed in Chapter Eleven, 26% of Americans feel isolated and disconnected from American society. Studies show that the more connected people are the happier they are. Conversely, those who are disconnected because of their economic well-being are more unhappy.

POINTS TO REMEMBER

- One measure that describes the health of a society is the amount of moral capital it possesses. Moral capital is the glue that holds a society together. Absent that glue, a nation becomes unhealthy and tribal.

- There are four contributors to moral capital: family, local community, moral community, and national or patriotic feelings

- The United States has always aspired to be a society with moral capital. At the time of its founding, the goals of the founders were expressed in the moral capital held by its people.

- Today our moral capital is in decline because the Postmodern world is uncertain and there is significant internal conflict.

CHAPTER FOURTEEN

THE WAY FORWARD

To be hopeful in bad times is not just foolishly romantic. It is based on the fact that human history is a history not only of cruelty but also of compassion, sacrifice, courage, kindness. **Howard Zinn**

This book was written to assert that the time has come for action against American Tribalism. Our detour from cultural stability must end before we irreparably damage American society and our political system. Unfortunately, no obvious solution presents itself and, because we are dealing with human behavior in a time of such polarity, the road to a better world promises to be hard. Even if there were an obvious solution, the divide in this nation is too great to span; lack of communication between opposing groups means no cooperation or compromise.

How can America return to its pre-tribal state? There is no simple answer but there are solutions and there is no time to lose in moving forward with them. An appropriate starting point would be academia, which has been corrupted by Postmodernism. Our universities and colleges have lost their historical mission to act as institutions that can moderate the ideas of mankind, subject them to criticism, and discard the ones that don't provide a benefit. The contemporary academic view embraces only Left-wing ideologies which are identity driven and divisive. No institution or political entity can have a corner on good ideas. All ideas must be considered for American society to reach a working consensus.

Get Americans talking

The most important project needed to mitigate Tribalism is to get the tribes talking. We have to find a way to unite Americans above the level of their tribes. American's are divided along ideological lines and there is no political middle. Those with a moderate point of view are neither activists, nor are they motivated to bridge the gap. Polls say they are angry at the antics of the extremists at both ends of the political spectrum.

Unfortunately, President Trump is a divider and not a person who unites. He uses a scorched-earth approach dealing with his enemies because that's his style. He attacks anyone who criticizes his efforts. What Trump has never understood is that the President is the symbol of the country and, in that role, he can do more than anyone to bring Americans together. It takes courtesy, friendliness, and compromise with the other side to make progress. The courtesy trait cannot be overstated, because politics is image and getting things done depends on protecting the adversary's image as well as one's own.

Fix Academia

Despite the entrenched position of Postmodernism in academia, efforts are underway to dislodge it. The Heterodox Academy[20] was created to try and open a dialog between all academics, regardless of differing points of view. The idea is to get people talking so they understand

---

[20] Heterodoxacademy.org

opposition perspectives and can engage in a rational debate of issues important to all Americans.

The Heterodox Academy will publish a list of universities that are focused on objective discourse versus those focused on an agenda-based subjective discourse. The tenure system was created to protect speech that is controversial, but necessary, for the testing of ideas. This tradition has been discarded in the last couple of decades, as academia moved toward a dogmatism reminiscent of the Spanish Inquisition. This new ranking system aims at a return to the historical role of academia by naming institutions that promote free speech.

Discussion has begun about developing new institutions of higher education based on the traditional principles that have served academia since the Enlightenment. These institutions would focus on free speech and the view of universities as centers for the exchange of all ideas, even controversial ones. There is an embryonic form of this on YouTube where intellectuals (the Intellectual Dark Web), are creating programs advocating for free speech in academia. Without ideologically biased university administrations to censor the dialog, free thought would be able to prosper.

If you think the corrupting of American universities is a problem too big to solve, remember the Protestant Reformation in Europe, which overcame all the power of the monarchs and the Catholic church, to change Western religion forever.

Find a new ideology for the Left

It's time for the Left to replace Postmodernism with another philosophical system. Postmodernism has no constructive method of solving the problems of humanity; its sole purpose is to act as critic of the modern world. Postmodernism cannot offer a path forward because it believes that grand narratives are obsolete. The time academia spends embracing Postmodernism is time wasted; it is time that could have been used to advance real intellectual ideas.

C.W, Mills (1916-1962), was a sociologist who helped launch the New Left movement in the 1960s. His statements about the hollowness of the welfare state have an ironic ring when applied to Postmodernism.

The end-of-ideology (a Postmodernist foundation), is a slogan of complacency, circulating among the prematurely middle-aged, centered in the present, and in the rich Western societies (American only in this case). In the final analysis, it also rests upon a disbelief in the shaping by men of their own futures — as history and as biography. It is a consensus of a few provincials about their own immediate and provincial situation. But the most immediately important thing about the "end of ideology" is that it *is* merely a fashion, and fashions change.

The end-of-ideology is on the way out because it stands for the refusal to work out an explicit political philosophy. And alert men everywhere today do feel the need of such a philosophy. What we should do is to continue directly to confront this need. In doing so, it may be useful to keep in mind that to have a working political philosophy means to have a philosophy that enables you to work.[21]

---

[21] C. Wright Mills. *Letter to the New Left.* (New Left Review, No. 5, September-October 1960), p. 3.

As Mills prophetically stated, political and philosophical movements depend on ideology for their motivation. Progress depends on the acceptance of a system that offers something better than ideologies operating today. The desire for something better creates the energy for change. Since Postmodernism offers no solution to fixing the problems of the Postmodern world, it should be abandoned in favor of an alternative that can benefit the human race.

Progressives and Postmodernism

The Progressive Movement has three parts; Postmodernist Progressives, Identity Politics Progressives, and Classic Progressives. The Postmodernist Progressives embrace the ideology they believe fits the Post-modern age. Whether they truly believe that is hard to know because they are trapped in their identity. Since the Humanities coopted Postmodernism to create a new use for itself, it can't go back. Where would it go?

Many Progressives dislike Postmodernism because it has inserted itself into their world and interfered with their attempts to carve out an ideological replacement for Socialism. Identity Politics Progressives are focused on the identity groups themselves and not the entire American society. The rest of the Left has remained Socialist or undecided. Progressives have always believed that efforts to improve American society must be based on a foundational ideology that begins with truth. Postmodernism's indifference to truth eliminates it as an acceptable belief system. How can an ideology constructed to criticize rather than improve be useful? Human knowledge depends a belief in consistent rules and laws. If there are no laws, there can only be chaos.

Absent an ideology, Progressives have become fatalists, suggesting that unless government implements collectivist programs, our society will collapse. In the 80's, the cry was "no more nukes," the 90's pushed radical environmentalism, so we could save the whales. The first decade of the 21st Century was focused on global warming. Now in the 2010's we have to become one global society to survive. These ideas are trendy but don't represent a permanent solution to our society's problems. In fact, they draw attention away from more serious problems.

In order to regain credibility, the Left needs to recover a strong, coherent and reasonable Liberalism. To do this, we need to out-discourse the postmodern-Left. We need to meet their oppositions, divisions and hierarchies with universal principles of freedom, equality and justice. There must be a consistency of liberal principles in opposition to all attempts to evaluate or limit people by race, gender or sexuality. We must address concerns about immigration, globalism and authoritarian identity politics currently empowering the Far-Right rather than calling people who express them "racist," "sexist" or "homophobic" and accusing them of wanting to commit verbal violence. We can do this whilst continuing to oppose authoritarian factions of the Right who genuinely are racist, sexist and homophobic, but can now hide behind a façade of reasonable opposition to the postmodern-Left.[22]

The oddity of Postmodernism's Influence in America

Why is it that Postmodernism had such a significant impact on American philosophy and culture and so little impact on the rest of the world? The Postmodernists were an interesting diversion, at best, in France, their native country. In Germany and England, the same result. Why would that be?

---

[22] Helen Pluckrose. *How French Intellectuals Ruined the West: Postmodernism and its Impact Explained.* (Aero Magazine, March 17, 2017), p. 11.

The answer lies somewhere in a comparison between European and American philosophy. The Europeans have a two-thousand-year history of philosophical thought. During the Enlightenment period, strong philosophical foundations were built in England, Germany, and France that are not easy to displace, particularly when the displacer is a movement that rejects all previous ideas.

America has no such history and, on occasion, invented its own philosophical forms. More important, because America is the world's largest economy, it exhibits the impact of economic advancement to a greater degree than the others. Modern media, including the Internet, advertising, and the consumer economy are a part of us for good or bad.

The sociological components of Postmodernism resonated better in America because they more accurately described the American mood.

Ending Tribalism across America

To remove Tribalism, we have to create moral capital that unites. It might come from moral communities, local communities, families, or it might come from patriotism based on a consensus that the American experiment still works and can endure.

Zeitgeist is a German word that describes a feeling that characterizes a period in history. It defines a spirit or mood that cannot be easily described or reduced to common language or comprehension. The zeitgeist changes subtly over time and often leads to events that are unpredictable. The collapse of the Soviet Union is an example of how the zeitgeist can take the world by surprise.

In the 1950s, in the United States, the zeitgeist had us putting World War II behind us, enjoying the peace, and taking advantage of all the new ways to make life easier. In the 1960s, our spiritual identity was centered around the Viet Nam War, which conflict dominated the decade. Student protests, against the establishment, and civil rights dominated the news. In the 1970s, the zeitgeist turned to distrust of government from the Watergate scandal and economic hardship from the oil crisis. Carter was elected as an outsider but was unsuccessful dealing with oil prices and high interest rates. In the Reagan years, the zeitgeist sensed a return to prosperity and good feelings generated by the collapse of the Soviet Union.

Today, the zeitgeist has ginned up a renewal of nationalistic sentiment among Americans who feel left out, as a response to globalism and multiculturalism. In Europe, a similar situation exists. As Angela Merkel has asserted, Multiculturalism is a failure. There is dissatisfaction with Globalism now because it attempts to homogenize the world and in doing so, labels some groups as non-participants in the new order. People in the non-participating groups are resisting.

During the rise of Globalism, Nationalism was labeled immoral, as if the word meant a return to Nazism. Nationalism in its pure form (non-hegemonic), adds moral capital that brings people closer as citizens of a single nation. Americans share our land, laws, and our history.

How do we move forward and end Tribalism? Our current social and political mindset is driven by adversarial feelings rather than congeniality. Something will have to poke the zeitgeist before it will reshape itself and take us someplace else. We can be encouraged by the fact that the zeitgeist can change direction in a relatively short period of time, which might mean we don't have to put up with the current political climate for too much longer.

Solutions that end Tribalism

In previous paragraphs, I described the overt steps that could be taken to counteract Tribalism. These included fixing Academia and discarding Postmodernism as a dead end. I see three ways Tribalism could abate, regardless of how much human effort is put toward that purpose. The first is fatigue. At some point the warring tribes will get tired of fighting, and the energy used in battle will be depleted. Perhaps the tribes will decide there are more important things to worry about, like the stability and prosperity of our republic. It's not possible to predict when this might happen, because the problem involves human beings, who defy logic. A zeitgeist change caused by fatigue could push the country into a more conciliatory mood.

A second solution could result from a shock that unites the country. An event, like 9/11, would make the petty arguments of political ideology inconsequential. One unfortunate legacy of 9/11 was that the Iraq war came too soon after the attacks and destroyed the moral capital that had resulted from it. Of course, there are other examples of national harmonizing in American history: Pearl Harbor, and the Confederate attack on Fort Sumter serving as examples. Because the attack on Pearl Harbor led to a four-year World

War, the time span was long enough to drastically change the country and push it in a new direction. As useful as this kind of shock-driven unity might be, it's not something we would wish on our nation.

The third way to end Tribalism would occur if bridges were built between the tribes, using communication to break down animosity. We all know that cordial conversation between people with differing views can lead to calmer rhetoric and greater understanding. Bridges built this way would strengthen moral capital; opponents could cross the ideological divide and find common ground. One way for this to happen is consensus in Congress about programs that matter to all the American people, rather than just focusing upon special interest groups. If Americans could see their government functioning as they believe it should, working for the benefit of all of us, the tension level would abate within the tribes. Unfortunately, this will not happen before the end of the Trump presidency. Successful or not, Trump is too divisive to get the Left talking to the Right. The Left is obsessed with destroying Trump to the point of irrationality, and it would take a change in Republican leadership to calm the waters.

In Chapter Two, we discussed the Enlightenment. One of its hallmarks was the emphasis on individualism. That belief is obscured and all but hidden in the United States today. Groups and Collectivism dominate. It's time for the individual to rise again and destroy the curse of tribal ghoulishness. It's the individual who has the most control over the future of our country because he has control over himself. The individual can decide to be open-minded, caring, friendly, and understanding; no one can stop that. People must look inward and make themselves stakeholders for change. Each new stakeholder produces a tiny piece of moral capital that collectively adds up to a force that can bring us back from the present abyss.

There is urgency here

For those who imagine we have plenty of time to fix Tribalism in the United States, it's time to re-imagine reality. China is out there ready to take over the world if we let them.

One of the limitations of democracy is a characteristic that makes it the most equitable political system, consensus. Consensus government is hard, because its success depends on the ability of the majority to agree on what needs to be done. Many times, there is no consensus. Democracies are adversarial, painful, and unsatisfying, but remain the best political systems for human society.

China is not a democracy. It's an authoritarian dictatorship. There is no need for consensus because the leadership decides how the government operates. The Chinese people have no say in how they are treated by their government. Dictatorships are very efficient because they don't have to govern based on election mandates.

China has the largest population of any country in the world, with a GDP two thirds the size of ours. Their goal is to control the world: the goal of all Communist ideologies. They have taken advantage of America on trade and built their economy on the backs of American workers. They indiscriminately steal our intellectual property and use it against us. They attack us through the Internet and disrupt our businesses. The Chinese are trying to sell us their computer equipment with spy chips inside. Those chips will gather information the Chinese will use to further their advantage.

We should not allow Chinese spy technology to enter the United States. [23]

America's stability depends on us having a razor-sharp focus on the world and the danger outside our borders. The continuing success of America in the world is more important than microaggressions, because the world is full of *macroaggressions.*

Another View

In *Bowling Alone,* Robert Putnam discussed the problem of lost social capital (my term is moral capital). He looked for historical analogs that could be useful, and chose the Progressive Era of 1870-1910 as the most appropriate example. Putnam spent many pages discussing how the Progressive Era was similar to contemporary America. During the Progressive Era, the debate was whether grassroots efforts or professional (government), action could do a better job at fixing problems. Professional approaches won the battle because the Federal government was seen as the only entity with enough power to force difficult social

---

[23] Bloomberg News. The Big Hack: How China Used a Tiny Chip to Infiltrate U.S. Companies. October 4, 2018.

changes to be made. Putnam noted that the Progressive Era featured an enormous uptick in social organizations, indicating that Americans felt shared interests could project influence for change. He asserted that the same behavior today could help bring Americans together again.

As I see it, the difference between then and now is politics. Since the political parties are deadlocked and tribal, there is no consensus on how our government can intervene to fix Tribalism in the United States. The government cannot become an agent for change until it is given direction by the American people, so it is the American people who must lead us forward individually or in groups. Human history says there are always people motivated for change. Those individuals have Progressive views. The momentum needed to Tribalism may have to come from the Left, but that can't happen unless they renew a working relationship with the Right that can be used to push the country forward.

POINTS TO REMEMBER

- **Solution number one. Fix Academia**

  Despite the entrenched position of Postmodernism in academia, efforts are underway to dislodge it.

- **Solution number two. Replace Postmodernism**

  Academia might return to its former self if Postmodernism were replaced with another philosophical system. That system would require an ideology the Left can use to reassume its traditional role.

- To fix Tribalism, we must create moral capital that unites us, regardless of our diversity. It might come from a moral community, local community, or family, or it might come from patriotism. We need to reach an agreement that the American experiment still works and can endure if the country can come together.

- Tribalism may go away on its own because of fatigue or a shock to the United States.

- Tribalism may go away if Americans can make an effort to communicate across tribes in order to solve the country's problems.

- Americans need to work on this problem. Wasting time over ideological extremes is not an acceptable diversion.

GLOSSARY

1. **Anarchism** – a political philosophy that advocates self-governed societies based on voluntary, cooperative institutions, rejecting unjust hierarchy. Absence of government.

2. **Capitalism** – an economic system that relies on the free exchange of goods between individuals and organizations. Value and prices are set by the market, so it is the interest of market players to be efficient in the production of goods, which will maximize their profits.

3. **Collectivism** – the belief that society is best structured to benefit groups rather than individuals. Collectivists constructed the Socialist model as a solution to economic inequality.

4. **Cosmopolitanism** – the belief that some ideas of value apply to the entire world as opposed to parts of it. It also embraces the idea that all humanity is a single community.

5. **Egalitarianism** – describes a society which grants equal status for all individuals. There is no hierarchy. Primitive man lived in egalitarian groups before the advent of agriculture.

6. **Empiricism** – is the philosophical idea that information comes to use through our senses, which provides our connection to the outside world. The senses are not always reliable, so our perceptions may not necessarily tell us the truth.

7. **Existentialism** – was a philosophical belief system most commonly associated with Jean Paul Sartre in the mid-20th Century. Existentialists believed that that the world exists in the mind of the individual and nothing else matters. Man is responsible for and in control of his own destiny.

8. **Fallibilism** – is a view of the scientific method that overcomes the absence of absolute truth. It allows science to accept experimental findings as true even though they can't be proved with certainty.

9. **Fascism** – a radical authoritarian political system based on collectivist (group) principles. Fascism is an example of totalitarianism.

10. **Humanism** – was a set of ideas that appeared during the early Renaissance period. Those ideas emphasized the value of human beings and argued against a focus on divine or supernatural matters.

11. **Idealism** – is a philosophical belief system that holds reality is constructed in the human mind. Objects outside the mind cannot be known.

12. **Liberalism** – 3 types based on the definition changing over time.

Classical Liberalism – a center piece to the Enlightenment, is a political system that is focused on the individual versus the group. Individuals are given the freedom to pursue their own success by selling their skills to the highest bidder. The market determines their value. Government performs basic functions but does not interfere in the market.

American or Modern Liberalism – a radical departure from Classical Liberalism and setup by Franklin Roosevelt in the 1930s. Roosevelt broke with unions and befriended Capitalists, so he could use the American economy to finance a welfare state. By the 1970s, the welfare state had become discredited and Liberalism fell out of favor.

Neoliberalism – created by Conservatives in the 1970s, this was a new way of looking at Libertarianism. It emphasized the sanctity of markets and that government should not interfere with them. Government should encourage national competitiveness as its goal and remove all barriers to trade, investment, and international financial transactions. The result of economic interdependence in the context of a world economy will be prosperity and world peace.

13. **Libertarianism** – an economic model that attempts to create as free an operating market as possible. In other words, a system with minimal government and no government interference in markets. Libertarians oppose foreign policy and foreign aid.

14. **Logical Positivism** – a theory that the only philosophical questions that matter can be answered using logical analysis.

15. **Marxism** – the theory of economic socialism developed by Karl Marx. Marx believed that the repression of a working class by their managers would eventually lead to a revolt against the government and generate a Socialist system.

16. **Materialism** – is a philosophical concept that nothing exists except matter and its movements.

17. **Mercantilism** – is the economic concept of trade and the sale of goods. It began at the time of global trading in the 15th Century. Its objective was to find new markets for trade, including both the importing and exporting of goods.

18. **Multiculturalism** – refers to a society that accepts and supports citizens from multiple cultures and encourages the retention of their identities. Multiculturalists believe that mixing cultures is good for society and leads to greater tolerance.

19. **Nationalism** – enthusiasm toward one's country as a model for the world. The pride that goes with being part of a specific culture as opposed to other cultures.

20. **Nativism** – the belief that native born members of a culture must have their interests protected against immigrants.

21. **Pluralism** – the belief that a culture benefits when it is made up of individuals from many cultures.

22. **Positivism** – a philosophical system that believes that every assertion can be scientifically verified by mathematics and logic.

23. **Postmodernism** – is a philosophical system introduced into the United States in the late 1970s. It seeks to explain the fragmentation and chaos of the late 20th Century as due to consumerism, expansion of mass media, and accelerated communications. Postmodernists suggest the ideas of the Enlightenment are outdated and need to be replaced by a new system that more accurately explains the world.

24. **Post-Structuralism** – attacks Structuralism as false and takes the position that there is no innate structure in the world. Concepts and ideas are socially constructed and do not tell us anything about the real world.

25. **Pragmatism** – a philosophical system that emphasizes the validity of objects to be based on how they behave in nature. Observing the characteristics of an object, makes the object real.

26. **Rationalism** – the belief that truth can be determined through contemplation and knowledge rather than religious beliefs or emotions.

27. **Realism** – the philosophical concept that reality exists outside of the human mind.

28. **Romanticism** – was a period in the first half of the 19th Century, when there was a strong reaction against the Enlightenment, based on the feeling that it had produced a world full of science and business, ignoring the aesthetic aspects of life. Romantics worshiped nature, the arts, and the validity of human emotional responses.

29. **Socialism** – is a political system in which the government controls the means of production rather than private industry. The purpose of this structure is to distribute wealth more evenly among the population so all members of the society have an equal share.

30. **Structuralism** – is a 20th Century philosophical belief system that the world consists of structures that describe the interaction between people and

things. In order to understand those structures, one most analyze patterns within them.

31. **Transcendentalism** – is an American philosophical system created by Ralph Waldo Emerson in response to the Romantic Movement. Emerson believed that isolation in nature can provide a connection to divinity, which is expressed in nature. That connection transcends the conformity of everyday life.

32. **Tribalism** – the tendency for groups to revert to smaller organizations when they become uncomfortable with larger organizations. Tribalism occurs when individuals believe larger organizations are failing, or have failed, to satisfy their people.

33. **Universalism** – a concept that there are ideas that connect all people. Implementing those ideas would make the world a better place.

BIBLIOGRAPHY

Antonio, Robert J. 2000. *After Postmodernism: Reactionary Tribalism*. American Journal of Sociology. Vol. 106 No. 1 (July) pp. 40-87.

Atkinson, Elizabeth. 2002. *Postmodernism and Social Change*. British Journal of Sociology of Education. Vol. 23 No. 1 (March), pp. 73-87.

Aust, Stephen. 1985. *Baader-Meinhof.* Translated by

Anthea Bell, 1987. Oxford, Oxford University Press.

Berlin, Isaiah. 1973. *The Counter-Enlightenment*. Essay.

Bernstein, Mary. 2005. *Identity Politics*. Annual Review of Sociology, Volume 31, pp. 47-74.

Best, Steven and Kellner, Douglas. 1998. *Postmodern Politics and the Battle for the Future*. New Political Science. Vol. 20 No. 3 (September) pp. 283-299.

Bloomberg News. The Big Hack: How China Used a Tiny Chip to Infiltrate U.S. Companies. October 4, 2018.

Bohannan, Paul. 1963. *Social Anthropology*. New York: Holt, Rinehart and Winston.

Brown, Doug. *An Institutionalist Look at Postmodernism*. Journal of Economic Issues, Vol. 25, No. 4 (December, 1991), pp. 1089-1104

Burnham, James. *Suicide of the West: An Essay on the Meaning and Destiny of Liberalism*. New York, Encounter Books.

Burns, James MacGregor. 2013. *Fire and Light: How the Enlightenment Transformed Our World*. New York, St. Martin's Press.

Cahoone, Lawrence. 1996. *From Modernism to Postmodernism. An Anthology*. Malden, Massachusetts, Blackwell Publishing.

Citrin, Jack, Sears, David O., Muste, Christopher, and Cara Wong. *Multiculturalism in American Public Opinion*. British Journal of Political Science, Vol. 31, No. 2 (April 2001), pp. 247-275

Derrida, Jacques. 1972 *Positions*. Translated by Alan Bass, 1981. Chicago, University of Chicago Press.

Derrida, Jacques. 2016. *Of Grammatology*. Translated by Gayatri Chakrovorty Spivak. Baltimore, Johns Hopkins University Press.

Eagleton, Terry. 1996. *The Illusions of Postmodernism*. Oxford, Blackwell Publishers.

Edwards, Mickey. 2012. *American Tribalism*. Chapter in *The Parties Versus the People*. New Haven, Yale University Press.

Epstein, Barbara. 1995. *Political Correctness and Collective Powerlessness*. Chapter from book titled *Cultural Politics* by Marcy Darnovsky, Barbara Epstein, Richard Flacks. Philadelphia, Temple University Press.

Epstein, Barbara. 1997. *Postmodernism and the Left*. New Politics, V. 6 No. 2, No. 22, (Winter).

Fichte, Johann Gottlieb. 1792. *Attempt at a Critique of All Revelation*. Edited by Alan Wood. Translated by Garrett Green. Cambridge, Cambridge University Press. 2012.

Fichte, Johann Gottlieb. 1807. *Addresses to the German Nation*. Translated by R.F. Jones and G.H. Turnbull. Chicago, University of Chicago Press, 1922. pp. 136-138 and 143-45.

Friedan, Betty. 2013. *The Feminine Mystique*. New York, W.W. Norton & Company.

Feuchtwanger, Edgar. 2002. *Bismarck*. London, Routledge Press.

Fukuyama, Francis. 2011. *The Origins of Political Order, from Pre-human Times to the French Revolution*. New York: Farrar, Straus, and Giroux.

Foucault, Michel. 2006. *The Will to Knowledge*. London, Penguin Books.

Fukuyama, Francis. 2014. *Political Order and Political Decay, from the Industrial Revolution to the Globalization of Democracy*. New York: Farrar, Straus, and Giroux.

Gabardi, Wayne. 2001. *1 – The Modern-Postmodern Debate and Its Legacy*. Chapter 1 of Negotiating Postmodernism. Minneapolis, University of Minnesota Press.

Greene, Thomas. 1974. *Comparative Revolutionary Movements*. New York: Prentice-Hall.

Gross, Paul R, Levitt, Norman, and Lewis, Martin W. Eds. 1996. *The Flight from Science and Reason*. New York, New York Academy of Sciences.

Haidt, Jonathan. 2012. *The Righteous Mind, Why Good People are Divided by Politics and Religion*. New York: Pantheon Books.

Hassan, Ihab. 1998. *Postmodernism Revisited: A Personal Account*. Amerikastudien, American Studies, Vol. 43 No. 1, Media and Cultural Memory, pp. 143-153.

Hauser, Marc D. 2006. *Moral Minds. How Nature Designed our Universal Sense of Right and Wrong*. New York: Harper Collins.

Hawkins, Stephen, Yudkin, Daniel, Juan-Torres, Miriam, and Dixon, Tim. 2018. *Hidden Tribes: A Study of America's Polarized Landscape*. Publisher - More in Common.

Hayek, F.A. 2007. *The Road to Serfdom*. London: University of Chicago Press.

Herder, Johann Gottfried. 1772. *A Treatise on the Origin of Language*. Edited and translated by Michael M. Forster, University of Chicago, 2002.

Herder, Johann Gottfried. 1776. *Outline of a Physical History of Humanity*. Edited and translated by T. Churchill, Bergman Publishers, New York, 1966.

Hicks, Stephen R.C. 2004. *Explaining Postmodernism. Skepticism from Rousseau to Foucault*. Ockham's Razor Publishing.

Horkheimer, Max 1937. *Traditional and Critical Theory*. Publisher unknown.

Horkheimer, Max, 1982. *Critical Theory*, New York: Seabury Press; reprinted Continuum: New York.

Horkheimer, Max and Adorno, Theodore. 2002. *Dialectic of the Enlightenment: Philosophical Fragments*. Edited by Gunzelin Schmid Noerr. Stanford, Stanford University Press.

Hughes, John A., Martin, Peter J., and Sharrock, W.E. 1995 *Understanding Classical Sociology: Marx, Weber, Durkheim.* London, Sage Publications.

Johnson, Paul. 1977. *Enemies of Society.* London: Weidenfeld & Nicolson.

Johnson, Paul. 1983. *Modern Times*: The World from the Twenties to the Eighties. New York: Harper and Row.

Kant, Immanuel. 1784. *What is Enlightenment?* Translated by Ted Humphrey. Indianapolis, Hackett Publishing, 1992.

Kant, Immanuel. 1784. *Idea for a History with a Cosmopolitan Aim.* Essay.

Kornhauser, William. 1959. *The Politics of Mass Society.* Glencoe, Illinois: The Free Press.

Kuhn, Thomas S. 1962. *The Structure of Scientific Revolutions.* Chicago, University of Chicago Press.

Lavine, Thelma Z. *Postmodernism and American Pragmatism.* The Journal of Speculative Philosophy, New Series, Vol. 7, No. 2 (1993), pp. 110-113

Link, Arthur S. 1967. American Epoch. A History of the United States since the 1890s. New York: Alfred A. Knopf.

Locke, John. 1790. *The Second Treatise of Government.* Project Gutenberg, 2010.

Maisel, Sandy. 2012. *The Negative Consequences of Uncivil Political Discourse*. Political Science and Politics, V. 45 No. 3 (July) pp. 405-411.

Marcuse, Herbert. 2002. *The One-Dimensional Man: Studies in the Ideology of Advanced Industrial Society*. New York and London, Routledge Classics.

Marx, Karl. 2012. *Das Kapital*. Chicago: Dragan Nicolic, Aristeus Books.

Marx, Karl, and Engels, Fredrich. 1848. *The Communist Manifesto*. Marx/Engels Selected Works, Vol. One, Progress Publishers, Moscow, 1969, pp. 98-137.

Marx, Karl and Engels, Fredrich. *Marx/Engels Selected Works*, Volume Three, p. 13 - 30 Publisher: Progress Publishers, Moscow, 1970

McMahon, Darrin M. 2001. *Enemies of the Enlightenment: The French Counter-Enlightenment and the Making of Modernity*. Oxford, Oxford University Press.

Mignet, F.A.M. 1912. *History of the French Revolution 1789-1814*. London: G. Bell.

Mills, C. Wright. 1960. *Letter to the New Left*. New Left Review, No. 5, September-October 1960.

Nairn, Tom and James, Paul. 2005. *Global Matrix: Nationalism, Globalism, and State-Terrorism*. London, Pluto Press.

Nettels, Curtis P. 1963. *The Roots of American Civilization. A History of American Colonial Life*. New York: Appleton-Century-Crofts.

Nozick, Robert. 1974. *Anarchy, State, and Utopia*. New York, Basic Books.

Orend, Brian, 1971. Kant's Just War Theory. Journal of the History of Philosophy. Volume 37, number 2, pp. 323-353.

Pinker, Steven. 2002. *The Blank Slate. The Modern Denial of Human Nature*. New York: Penguin Putnam.

Pluckrose, Helen 2017. *How French "Intellectuals" Ruined the West: Postmodernism and its Impact Explained*. Aero Magazine Online March 17, 2017.

Poster, Mark. 1984. *Foucault, Marxism, & History: Mode of Production versus Mode of Information*. Cambridge, Polity Press.

Pritchett, Wendell E. 2005. *Identity Politics, Past and Present*. International Labor and Working-Class History, No. 67, Class and the Politics of Identity, (Spring) pp. 33-41.

Public Religion Research Institute. 2018. *White Evangelical Support for Trump at an All-time High.* PRRI April 18, 2018.

Rawls, John. 1971/1999. *Theory of Justice.* Cambridge, Harvard University Press
Riesman, David. 1961. *The Lonely Crowd.* New Haven, Yale University Press.

Robertson, John. 2015. *The Enlightenment: A Very Short Introduction.* Oxford, Oxford University Press.

Rorty, Richard, Amélie Oksenberg, and James Schmidt. 2009. *Kant's Idea for a Universal History with a Cosmopolitan Aim – A Critical Guide.* Cambridge, Cambridge University Press.

Rorty, Richard. 1991. *Objectivity, Relativism, and Truth.* Cambridge, Cambridge University Press.

Rorty, Richard. 1991 *Essays on Heidegger and Others.* Cambridge, Cambridge University Press.

Sanbonmatsu, John. 2004. *The Postmodern Prince.* New York, Monthly Review Press.

Sanbonmatsu, John. 2006. *Postmodernism and The Corruption of The Academic Intelligentsia.* Socialist Register, Volume 42.

Sasse, Ben. 2018. Essay from Them: *Why we hate each other*. New York, St. Martin's Press.

Schutze, Martin. 1944. *Johann Gottfried Herder August 25, 1744 – December 18, 1803: His Significance in the History of Thought*. Monatshefte für Deutschen Unterricht, Vol. 36, No. 6 October, pp. 257-287.

Service, Elman R. 1962. *Primitive Social Organization. An Evolutionary Perspective*. New York: Random House.

Service, Elman R. 1975. *The Origins of the State and Civilization. The Process of Cultural Evolution*. New York: W.W. Norton.

Shapiro, Ian. 2003. *The Moral Foundations of Politics*. New Haven: Yale University Press.

Shepard, Lindsay. 2018. *Exposing Grad School*. YouTube Video. November 5, 2018.

Smith, Stephen. 2012. *Political Philosophy*. New London, Yale University Press.

Sombart, Werner. 1915. Merchants and Heroes. Publisher unknown

Spengler, Oswald. 1991. *The Decline of the West*. Oxford, Oxford University Press.

Spengler, Oswald. 2013. *Prussianism and Socialism.* Oxford, Madampatti, Coimbatore, India. Isha Books.

Spengler, Oswald. 2002. *Man and Technics.* Oxford, Honolulu, University Press of the Pacific.

Stace, W.T. 1955. The Philosophy of Hegel. A Systematic Exposition. New York, New York, Dover Publications.

Sullivan, Andrew. 2017. American Wasn't Built for Humans. New York Magazine, September 18, 2017.

Turiel, Elliot. 2002. *The Culture of Morality.* Cambridge: Cambridge University Press.

United States Declaration of Independence, July 4, 1776.

van der Laan, J.M. 2009. *Johann Gottfried Herder on War and Peace.* Monatshefte, Vol. 101, No. 3 (Fall), pp. 335-346.

Van Zon, Hans. 2013. *The Unholy Alliance Between Neoliberalism and Postmodernism.* Vlaams Marxistisch Tudschrift. Jaargang 47 number 2. (Zomer).

Vedder, Richard. 2018. *"Kill all the Administrators" (Not really).* Forbes online, May 10, 2018.

Victor, Pierre quoted in Miller, James. 1993. The Passion of Michel Foucault. Cambridge, Harvard University Press

Voltaire, 1962. *Philosophical Dictionary*, trans. and ed. Peter Gay, 2 vols. New York: Basic Books.

Wende, Peter. 2005. *A History of Germany*. Hampshire, Palgrave MacMillan.

Whitehead, Alfred North and Russell, Bertrand. 2011. *Principia Mathematica*. New York, Rough Draft Printing.

Woods, Tim. 1999. *Beginning Postmodernism*. Manchester, Manchester University Press.

INDEX

A

agriculture, 46, 48-49, 73

Althusser, Louis, 164

Analytic Philosophy, 158, 160, 184, 187

Anarchism, 39, 107, 117

B

Baader, Andreas, 140–142

Bacon, Francis, 391–40

Bakunin, Mikhail, 107–108

Bonaparte, Napoleon, 53, 74

Brandt, Willy, 131

C

Calvinism, 35, 122, 243, 248–249

Carnegie, Andrew, 147, 182

Classicism, 61

Collectivism, 5, 9, 18, 42, 93–97, 116-117, 283

Comte, Auguste, 151

Consumerism, 21, 81, 89-91, 177

Critical Theory, 125–127, 144, 215

Culturalism, 193

D

Darwin, Charles, 74, 91, 180

Dawkins, Richard, 179

Deconstruction, 174

Defenestration, 241

Derrida, Jacques, 143, 165, 173-176
Descartes, Rene, 36, 40, 52, 163
Diversity, 21, 226
Dualism, 174–177

E

Eagleton, Terry, 193
Egalitarianism, 57
Emerson, Ralph Waldo, 180
Empiricism, 37, 150, 181
Engels, Friedrich, 93, 108-109
Environmentalism, 88, 208, 276
Epstein, Barbara, 187, 192
Erasmus, 34-35
Evolution, 74, 180
Existentialism, 38, 163-164

F

Fallibilism, 62-63
Fascist, 124, 205–206
Feminists, 91, 187, 208, 210–212, 216
Fichte Johann Gottlieb, 101–104, 116
Foucault, Michel, 140, 143, 165, 171–176
187–188, 195
Fourier, Charles, 105-106
Frankfurt School, 124–125, 127-128, 132–135, 139,144-
145

G

Galileo, 40, 218
Genocide, 76, 162, 260

Globalism, 2, 277, 280
Godesberg Program, The, 130-131, 144

H
Hayek, Friedrich, 201–202
Hegel, Georg Wilhelm Friedrich, 64-65, 94, 104, 108, 112, 155
Heidegger, Martin, 138, 155–160, 163, 173
Herder, Johann, 98–100, 103–104, 116
Hobbes, Thomas, 42
Horkheimer, Max, 125–127, 134
Humanism, 33, 159

I
Idealism, 101, 108, 193
Individualism, 38, 70, 93-94, 111, 167
Industrialization, 45, 91
Internationalism, 26, 114
Irrationalism, 65, 142

J
Jünger, Ernst, 113

K
Kant, Immanuel, 37, 63, 94, 96–98, 101, 102, 104, 116, 127, 155, 166
Khrushchev, Nikita, 129
Kierkegaard, Soren, 65, 155, 160, 164
Kuhn, Thomas, 158

L

Levitt, Norman, 218
Libertarian, 107, 183–185, 209
Luther, Martin, 35, 239
Lyotard, Jean Francois, 143, 170–171, 176

M
Marcuse, Herbert, 133, 135, 143, 145
Marxism, 108, 114, 127, 134, 138, 167
170–171, 177, 213
Maslow, Abraham, 230–232, 256
Materialism, 127, 131
McIntyre, Alasdair, 185-186
Meinhof, Ulrike, 140–142, 145
Mercantilism, 45, 47, 72
Merkel, Angela, 280
Modernism, 90, 170, 216
Multiculturalism, 22–23, 138, 194, 205, 232, 280

N
Neoconservatism, 201
Neoliberalism,201–203
Newton, Isaac, 40–41
Nietzsche, Friedrich, 65–66, 155, 159–161,
166
Nihilism, 169, 177
Nozick, Robert, 185

P
Patriotism, 11, 256, 259, 262, 265, 278, 287
Peirce, Charles Sanders, 62
Phenomenology, 155–157, 158–160, 163

Philosophe, 53–55

Plenge, Johann, 112

Positivism, 139, 150–156, 160, 182

Poststructuralism, 165, 167

Pragmatism, 181–182

Progressive, 20–23, 25, 61, 78, 163, 182, 192, 194, 200–201, 205, 208, 210, 224–226, 250–251, 275–276, 285–286

R

Rational thinking, 36

Rationalism, 36–38, 59, 61, 137–138, 142

Rawls, John, 183–185, 195

Reformation, 35, 72, 273

Renaissance, 45, 70–71

Romantic movement, 58, 60–62, 67, 180

Rousseau, Jean-Jacques, 18-19, 42, 94–96, 104, 116, 163, 173

S

Sartre, John Paul, 164, 290

Schleiermacher, Friedrich, 65

Schopenhauer, Arthur, 65, 155

Skepticism, 48, 63, 155

Solzhenitsyn, Alexander, 166

Sombart, Werner, 113-114

Spengler, Oswald, 112–113

Structuralism, 164–167, 293-294

T

Terrorism, 141–143
Thoreau, Henry David, 180
Totalitarianism, 167, 202
Transcendentalism, 180, 195

U
Universalism, 24, 114, 138, 295
Utopian, 73, 105, 109–110, 117

W
Whitehead, Alfred North, 152
Wittgenstein, Ludwig, 153

Z
Zeitgeist, 60, 279–281

www.ingramcontent.com/pod-product-compliance
Lightning Source LLC
Chambersburg PA
CBHW060309030426
42336CB00011B/985